SIDE by SIDE

Extra

Book & eBook 3

Expanded Grammar

Self-Tests & Skill Checks

Digital FunZone & Audio

Steven J. Molinsky • Bill Bliss

Illustrated by Richard E. Hill

Side by Side Extra Book & eBook 3

Pearson Education, 10 Bank Street, White Plains, NY 10606

Staff credits: The people who make up the **Side by Side Extra** team, representing content creation, design, manufacturing, marketing, multimedia, project management, publishing, rights management, and testing are Pietro Alongi, Allen Ascher, Rhea Banker, Elizabeth Barker, Lisa Bayrasli, Elizabeth Carlson, Jennifer Castro, Tracey Munz Cataldo, Diane Cipollone, Aerin Csigay, Victoria Denkus, Dave Dickey, Daniel Dwyer, Wanda España, Oliva Fernandez, Warren Fischbach, Pam Kirshen Fishman, Nancy Flaggman, Patrice Fraccio, Irene Frankel, Aliza Greenblatt, Lester Holmes, Janet Johnston, Caroline Kasterine, Barry Katzen, Ray Keating, Renee Langan, Jaime Lieber, Amy McCormick, José Antonio Méndez, Julie Molnar, Alison Pei, Pamela Pia, Stuart Radcliffe, Jennifer Raspiller, Kriston Reinmuth, Mary Perrotta Rich, Tania Saiz-Sousa, Katherine Sullivan, Paula Van Ells, Kenneth Volcjak, and Wendy Wolf.

Contributing authors: Laura English, Meredith Westfall

Text composition: TSI Graphics, Inc.

Illustrations: Richard E. Hill

Photo credits: Page 33 (top) epa european pressphoto agency b.v./Alamy, (bottom) Hulton Archive/Getty Images; p. 34 (top left) Karel Miragaya/123RF, (top middle) Dan Himbrechts/Bloomberg/Getty Images, (top right) Reuters/Corbis, (middle left) Rolf Hicker Photography/Alamy, (middle) David R. Frazier Photolibrary, Inc./Alamy, (middle right) Vespasian/Alamy, (bottom) Ned Frisk/Blend Images/Getty Images; p. 65 (top right) Sorbis/Shutterstock, (top middle right) Reuters Photographer/Reuters, (middle right) Bill Varie/Corbis, (bottom left) Ian Lishman/Juice Images/Corbis (bottom middle) LookEngland/Alamy, (bottom right) Susan Steinkamp/Corbis; p. 66 (top left) AP Images, (top middle) blickwinkel/Alamy, (top right) Gordon Wiltsie/National Geographic Image Collection/Glow Images, (middle left) Greatstock Photographic Library/Alamy, (middle) Corbis/Glow Images, (middle right) Tom Williams/Roll Call/Newscom, (bottom) Shutterstock; p. 111 (top) Colorsport/Corbis, (bottom left) AF archive/Alamy, (bottom right) epa European pressphoto agency b.v./Alamy; p. 112 (top left) Ton Koene/SuperStock, (top middle) Eye Ubiquitous/SuperStock, (top right) BPA C Xinhua News Agency/Newscom, (middle left) ITAR-TASS/Newscom, (middle) Corbis Bridge/Alamy, (middle right) AFP/Getty Images/Newscom, (bottom) Jupiterimages/Exactostock/SuperStock; p. 145 Thomas Boehm/Alamy; p. 146 (US) Digital Vision/Photodisc/Getty Images, (Hindu) david pearson/Alamy, (Slovak) Magdalena Rehova/Alamy, (Korean) TOPIC PHOTO AGENCY IN/AGE Fotostock, (Romanian) Caroline Penn/Corbis, (musicians) Massimo Pizzocaro/Alamy, (confetti) kaphotokevm1/Fotolia, (petals) Purestock/Getty Images, (rice) elitravo/Shutterstock, (money) Jonathan Blair/Corbis, (candles) Cleve Bryant/PhotoEdit, Inc, (cake) Jeffrey Banke/Fotolia, (boat) Koichi Kamoshida/AsiaPac/Getty Images, (bouquet) Sergey Nivens/Shutterstock; p. 147 (top left) Stuart Jenner/Shutterstock, (top middle) Glow Images/SuperStock, (top right) ARENA Creative/Shutterstock, (bottom left) Deklofenak/Fotolia, (bottom middle left) Blend Images/Shutterstock, (bottom middle right) Jenkedco/Shutterstock, (bottom right) Mart of Images/Alamy.

The authors gratefully acknowledge the contributions of Pam Kirshen Fishman and Tina Carver in the development of the original **Side by Side** program.

Library of Congress Cataloging-in-Publication Data

Names: Molinsky, Steven J., author. | Bliss, Bill, author.
Title: Side by side extra : book & eBook / Steven J. Molinsky ; Bill Bliss.
Description: Third Edition. | White Plains, NY : Pearson Education, [2016] |
  Includes index.
Identifiers: LCCN 2015025510
Subjects: LCSH: English language--Conversation and phrase books. | English
  language--Textbooks for foreign speakers.
Classification: LCC PE1131 .M576 2016 | DDC 428.3/4--dc23
LC record available at http://lccn.loc.gov/2015025510

Side by Side Extra Book & eBook 3: ISBN 13 – 978-0-13-832166-6
32 2025

Side by Side Extra Book & eBook International 3: ISBN 13 – 978-0-13-430650-6

Printed in the United States of America

CONTENTS

1

Review:
Simple Present Tense
Present Continuous Tense
Subject & Object Pronouns
Possessive Adjectives
Time Expressions

- **Describing Habitual and Ongoing Activities**
- **Telling About Likes and Dislikes**
- **Describing Frequency of Actions**
- **Telling About Personal Background and Interests**

Vocabulary Preview

1 
2 
3 
4 
5 
6 
7 
8 
9 
10 
11 
12 

1. actor
2. dancer
3. driver
4. instructor
5. player
6. singer
7. skater
8. skier
9. swimmer
10. teacher
11. typist
12. violinist

They're Busy

Am	I	
Is	he / she / it	eating?
Are	we / you / they	

	I	am.
Yes,	he / she / it	is.
	we / you / they	are.

(I am)	I'm	
(He is)	He's	
(She is)	She's	
(It is)	It's	eating.
(We are)	We're	
(You are)	You're	
(They are)	They're	

A. Are you busy?

B. Yes, I am. I'm studying.

A. What are you studying?

B. I'm studying English.

1. Is Alan busy?
baking • cookies

2. Is Doris busy?
reading • the newspaper

3. Are your parents busy?
painting • the kitchen

4. Are you busy?
writing • a letter

5. Are you and Tom busy?
cooking • dinner

6. Is Ann busy?
knitting • a sweater

7. Is your brother busy?
ironing • his shirts

8. Are Mr. and Mrs. Garcia busy?
cleaning • their garage

9. Is Beethoven busy?
composing • a symphony

What Are They Doing?

Do	I we you they	eat?
Does	he she it	

Yes,	I we you they	do.
	he she it	does.

I We You They	eat.
He She It	eats.

A. What are you doing?

B. I'm practicing the piano.

A. Do you practice the piano very often?

B. Yes, I do. I practice the piano whenever I can.

1. What's Carol doing?
watch the news

2. What's Edward doing?
swim

3. What are you doing?
study math

4. What are Mr. and Mrs. Park doing?
exercise

5. What are you and your friend doing?
play Scrabble

6. What's Mrs. Anderson doing?
read poetry

7. What's Daniel doing?
play baseball with his daughter

8. What are you doing?
chat online with my friends

9.

Do You Like to Ski?

No, { I / we / you / they } don't. (do not)
No, { he / she / it } doesn't. (does not)

I'm not . . .
{ He / She / It } isn't . . . (is not)
{ We / You / They } aren't . . . (are not)

A. Do you like to ski?

B. No, I don't. I'm not a very good skier.

1. Does Richard like to sing?
singer

2. Does Brenda like to swim?
swimmer

3. Do Mr. and Mrs. Adams like to skate?
skaters

4. Does Arthur like to dance?
dancer

5. Do you like to type?
typist

6. Do you and your friend like to act?
actors

7. Does your grandmother like to drive?
driver

8. Do you like to play sports?
athlete

9. Does Howard like to cook?
cook

READING

PRACTICING

My sisters, my brother, and I are busy this afternoon. We're staying after school, and we're practicing different things.

I'm practicing soccer. I practice soccer every day after school. My soccer coach tells me I'm an excellent soccer player, and my friends tell me I play soccer better than anyone else in the school. I want to be a professional soccer player when I grow up. That's why I practice every day.

My sister Anita is practicing tennis. She practices tennis every day after school. Her tennis coach tells her she's an excellent tennis player, and her friends tell her she plays tennis better than anyone else in the school. Anita wants to be a professional tennis player when she grows up. That's why she practices every day.

My brother Hector is practicing the violin. He practices the violin every day after school. His music teacher tells him he's an excellent violinist, and his friends tell him he plays the violin better than anyone else in the school. Hector wants to be a professional violinist when he grows up. That's why he practices every day.

My sisters Jenny and Vanessa are practicing ballet. They practice ballet every day after school. Their ballet instructor tells them they're excellent ballet dancers, and their friends tell them they dance better than anyone else in the school. Jenny and Vanessa want to be professional ballet dancers when they grow up. That's why they practice every day.

READING *CHECK-UP*

Q & A

You're talking with the person who told the story on page 5. Using this model, create dialogs based on the story.

A. *What's your sister Anita* doing?
B. *She's* practicing *tennis*.
A. *Does she* practice very often?
B. Yes, *she does*. *She practices* every day after school.
A. *Is she a* good *tennis player*?
B. Yes, *she is*. *Her tennis instructor* says *she's* excellent, and *her* friends tell *her she plays tennis* better than anyone else in the school.

LISTENING

Listen and choose the correct answer.

1. a. I practice football.
   b. I'm practicing football.
2. a. Yes, I am.
   b. Yes, I do.
3. a. Yes, I am.
   b. Yes, I do.
4. a. She reads the newspaper.
   b. She's reading the newspaper.
5. a. My husband cooks.
   b. My husband is cooking.
6. a. No, they aren't.
   b. No, they don't.
7. a. Yes, when he grows up.
   b. Yes, when she grows up.
8. a. Yes, we do.
   b. Yes, you do.
9. a. Yes, they are.
   b. Yes, we are.
10. a. He's playing soccer.
    b. He wants to be a soccer player.

IN YOUR OWN WORDS

For Writing and Discussion

Tell about studying English.

Do you go to English class? Where?
When do you go to class?
What's your teacher's name?

When do you practice English?
How do you practice?
Who do you practice with?

How Often?

I	my	me
he	his	him
she	her	her
it	its	it
we	our	us
you	your	you
they	their	them

Time Expressions

every day/week/weekend/month/year
every morning/afternoon/evening/night
every Sunday/Monday/Tuesday/. . .
every Sunday morning/afternoon/evening/night
every January/February/March/. . .

once a / twice a / three times a } day/week/month/year

all the time

A. Who are you calling?

B. **I'm** calling **my** sister in San Francisco.

A. How often do you call **her**?

B. I call **her** every Sunday evening.

A. What are George and Herman talking about?

B. **They're** talking about **their** grandchildren.

A. How often do they talk about **them**?

B. They talk about **them** all the time.

1. Who is Mr. Tanaka calling?
son in New York

2. Who is Mrs. Kramer writing to?
daughter in the army

3. What are the students talking about?
teachers

4. Who is Lenny arguing with?
landlord

5. Who is Martha sending an e-mail to?
granddaughter in Orlando

6. Who is Mr. Crabapple shouting at?
employees

7. What are your parents complaining about?
telephone bill

8. What is George watching?
favorite TV talk show

9. Who is Little Red Riding Hood visiting?
grandmother

10.

How to Say It!

Asking for and Reacting to Information

A. Tell me, *where are you from*?
B. *I'm from Madagascar*.
A. { Oh. / Really? / Oh, really? / That's interesting. }

Practice the interactions on this page, using expressions for asking for and reacting to information.

INTERACTIONS *Sharing Opinions*

Talking about yourself:

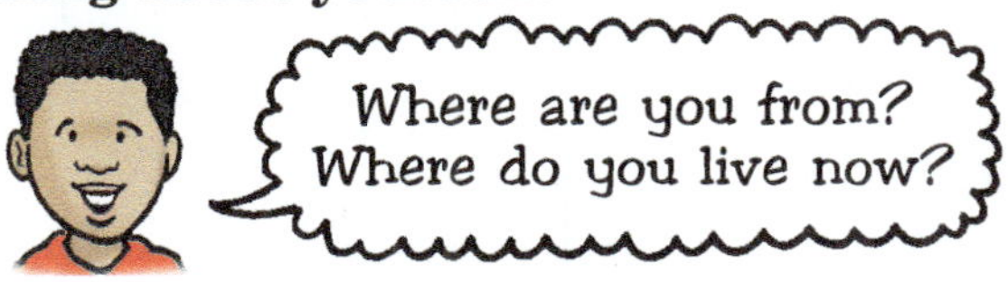

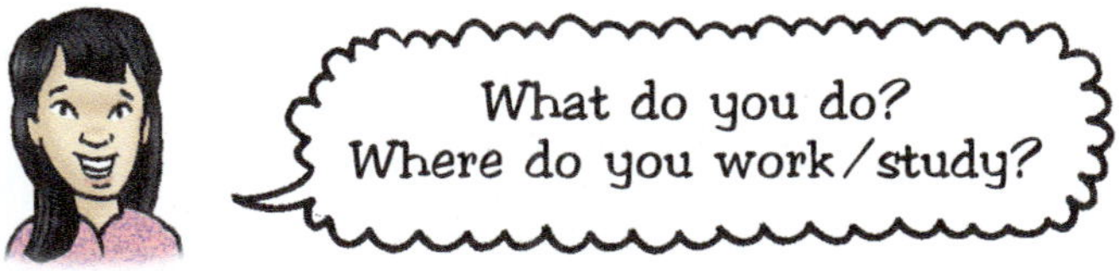

Talking about family:

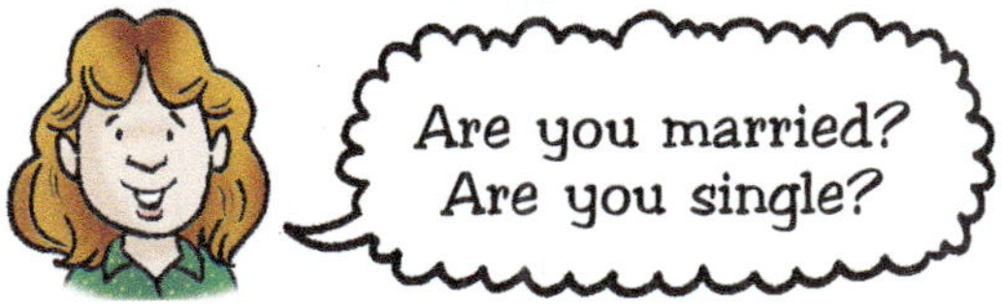

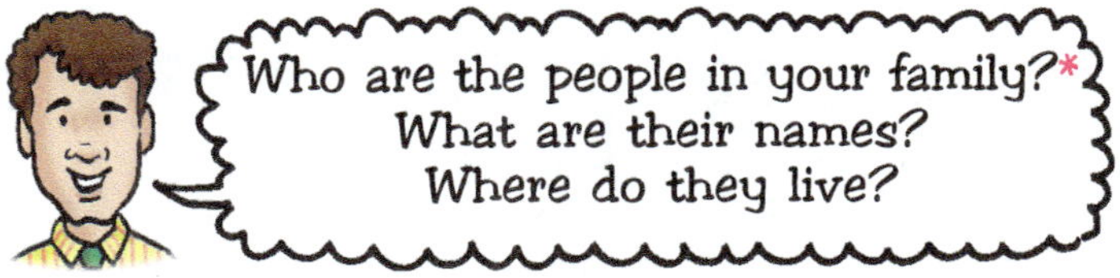

Talking about interests:

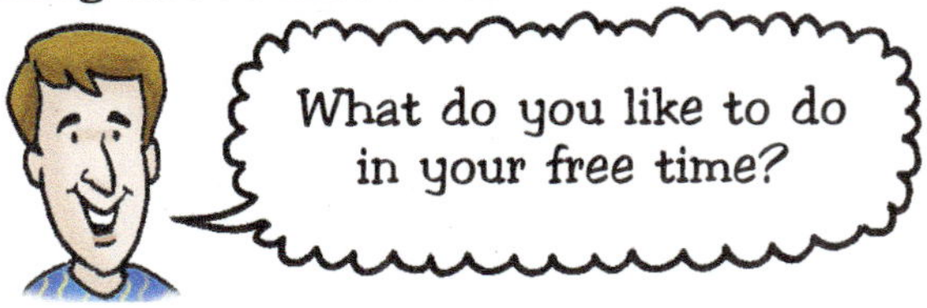

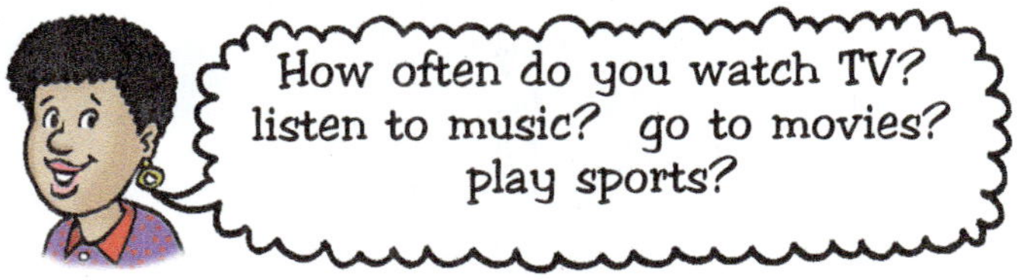

Practice conversations with other students. Get to know each other as you talk about yourselves, your families, and your interests.

* wife, husband, mother, father, daughter, son, sister, brother, grandmother, grandfather, granddaughter, grandson, aunt, uncle, cousin

Write in your journal about yourself, your family, and your interests.

PRONUNCIATION Reduced *are*

Listen. Then say it.

Who are you calling?

What are they talking about?

Where are you from?

What are you doing?

Say it. Then listen.

Who are you writing to?

What are they complaining about?

Where are they studying?

What are their names?

GRAMMAR FOCUS

Present Continuous Tense

(I am)	I'm	eating.
(He is) (She is) (It is)	He's She's It's	
(We are) (You are) (They are)	We're You're They're	

Am	I	eating?
Is	he she it	
Are	we you they	

To Be: Short Answers

Yes,	I	am.
	he she it	is.
	we you they	are.

No,	I'm	not.
	he she it	isn't.
	we you they	aren't.

Simple Present Tense

I We You They	eat.
He She It	eats.

Do	I we you they	eat?
Does	he she it	

Yes,	I we you they	do.
	he she it	does.

No,	I we you they	don't.
	he she it	doesn't.

Subject Pronouns	Possessive Adjectives	Object Pronouns
I	my	me
he	his	him
she	her	her
it	its	it
we	our	us
you	your	you
they	their	them

Choose the correct answer.

1. Mark is busy. (He irons He's ironing) his pants and shirts this morning.
2. My daughter (chats is chatting) online with her friends every day.
3. (We We're) watch (are our) favorite TV program every afternoon.
4. A. What (are our) Ann and Rita (do doing)?
   B. (They're Their) talking about (they're their) grandchildren.
5. Why (are do) your neighbors (argue arguing) with the landlord today?
6. (Is Does) your son (practice practicing) the piano every day?
7. (I'm calling I call) my cousins in Denver once a month.
8. A. (Is Does) your wife working today?
   B. No, she (is isn't). She (isn't doesn't) work on Saturday.

2

Review: Simple Past Tense (Regular and Irregular Verbs) Past Continuous Tense

- Reporting Past Activities
- Mishaps
- Difficult Experiences
- Describing a Trip

Vocabulary Preview

1. break – broke
2. buy – bought
3. cut – cut
4. eat – ate
5. fall – fell
6. go – went
7. hurt – hurt
8. lose – lost
9. meet – met
10. ride – rode
11. sing – sang
12. speak – spoke
13. swim – swam
14. teach – taught
15. write – wrote

Did They Sleep Well Last Night?

What did { I / he / she / it / we / you / they } do?

{ I / He / She / It / We / You / They } worked.

{ I / He / She / It } was / { We / You / They } were tired.

A. Did Emma sleep well last night?

B. Yes, she did. She was VERY tired.

A. Why? What did she do yesterday?

B. She worked in her garden all day.

1. *you*
study English

2. *Rick*
paint his apartment

3. *you and your brother*
wash windows

4. *Ms. Taylor*
teach

5. *Henry*
deliver pizzas

6. *Sarah*
write letters

7. *Matthew*
ride his bicycle

8. *the president*
meet important people

9.

Did Robert Shout at His Dog?

Yes/No, { I / he / she / it / we / you / they } did/didn't. (did not)

{ I / He / She / It } was/wasn't . . . (was not)

{ We / You / They } were/weren't . . . (were not)

A. Did Robert shout at his dog?

B. Yes, he did. He was angry.

A. Did Helen sleep well last night?

B. No, she didn't. She wasn't tired.

1. Did Howard fall asleep in class?
Yes, ____________. ____________ *bored.*

2. Did Amy take the plane to Rio?
No, ____________. ____________ *on time.*

3. Did you cry during the movie?
Yes, ____________. ____________ *sad.*

4. Did Brad do well on his exam?
No, ____________. ____________ *prepared.*

5. Did Frank and James forget their lines during the school play?
Yes, ____________. ____________ *nervous.*

6. Did you and your sister cover your eyes during the science fiction movie?
No, ____________. ____________ *scared.*

7. Did Abby finish her dinner?
Yes, ____________. ____________ *hungry.*

8. Did Timmy drink all his milk?
No, ____________. ____________ *thirsty.*

How Did Marty Break His Leg?

I He She It	was	working.
We You They	were	

A. How did Marty break his leg?

B. He broke it while he was snowboarding.

A. That's too bad!

1. How did Greta sprain her ankle?
play volleyball

2. How did Larry lose his wallet?
hike in the woods

3. How did Brian cut himself?
shave

4. How did Mr. and Mrs. Harper burn themselves?
prepare dinner

5. How did Stella rip her pants?
do her daily exercises

6. How did your grandfather trip and fall?
get off a bus

7. How did Peter poke himself in the eye?
talk on his cell phone

8. How did Marilyn cut herself?
chop onions

9. How did Timothy get a black eye?
fight with the kid across the street

10. How did Presto the Magician hurt himself?
practice a new magic trick

How to Say It!

Reacting to Bad News

Practice the conversations in this lesson again. React to the bad news in different ways.

READING

DIFFICULT EXPERIENCES

Ms. Henderson usually teaches very well, but she didn't teach very well this morning. In fact, she taught very badly. While she was teaching, the school principal was sitting at the back of the room and watching her. It was a very difficult experience for Ms. Henderson. She realized she wasn't teaching very well, but she couldn't do anything about it. She was too nervous.

Stuart usually types very well, but he didn't type very well today. In fact, he typed very badly. While he was typing, his supervisor was standing behind him and looking over his shoulder. It was a difficult experience for Stuart. He realized he wasn't typing very well, but he couldn't do anything about it. He was too upset.

The Baxter Boys usually sing very well, but they didn't sing very well last night. In fact, they sang very badly. While they were singing, their parents were sitting in the audience and waving at them. It was a difficult experience for the Baxter Boys. They realized they weren't singing very well, but they couldn't do anything about it. They were too embarrassed.

The president usually speaks very well, but he didn't speak very well this afternoon. In fact, he spoke very badly. While he was speaking, several demonstrators were standing at the back of the room and shouting at him. It was a difficult experience for the president. He realized he wasn't speaking very well, but he couldn't do anything about it. He was too angry.

READING *CHECK-UP*

Q & A

Ms. Henderson, Stuart, the Baxter Boys, and the president are talking with friends about their difficult experiences. Using this model, create dialogs based on the story on page 16.

A. You know . . . I didn't *teach* very well *this morning*.
B. You didn't?
A. No. In fact, I *taught* very badly.
B. That's strange. You usually *teach* VERY well. What happened?
A. While I was *teaching, the school principal was sitting at the back of the room and watching me.*
B. Oh. I bet that was a very difficult experience for you.
A. It was. I *was* very *nervous*.

MATCH

We often use colorful expressions to describe how we feel. Try to match the following expressions with the feelings they describe.

____ 1.	"My stomach is growling."	a.	angry
____ 2.	"I can't keep my eyes open."	b.	embarrassed
____ 3.	"I'm jumping for joy!"	c.	tired
____ 4.	"I'm seeing red!"	d.	nervous
____ 5.	"I'm feeling blue."	e.	scared
____ 6.	"I'm on pins and needles!"	f.	hungry
____ 7.	"I'm shaking like a leaf!"	g.	sad
____ 8.	"I'm ashamed to look at them straight in the eye."	h.	happy

LISTENING

Listen and choose the correct answer.

1. a. Yes, I did.
   b. Yes, I was.
2. a. Yes, they did.
   b. Yes, they were.
3. a. He played soccer.
   b. He was playing soccer.
4. a. No. I wasn't hungry.
   b. Yes. I wasn't hungry.
5. a. He lost his wallet.
   b. He was jogging in the park.
6. a. She was nervous.
   b. She was looking over my shoulder.
7. a. Yes. I was prepared.
   b. No. I was prepared.
8. a. I cut myself.
   b. I was too upset.

Tell Me About Your Vacation

1. **A.** Did you go to Paris?
   B. No, __we didn't__.
   A. Where __did you go__?
   B. __We went__ to Rome.

2. **A.** Did you get there by boat?
   B. No, ________.
   A. How ________?
   B. ________ by plane.

3. **A.** Did you stay in a big hotel?
   B. No, ________.
   A. What kind of ________?
   B. ________ a small hotel.

4. **A.** Did you eat in fancy restaurants?
   B. No, ________.
   A. Where ________?
   B. ________ cheap restaurants.

5. **A.** Did you speak Italian?
   B. No, ________.
   A. What language ________?
   B. ________ English.

6. **A.** Did you take many pictures?
   B. No, ________.
   A. How many ________?
   B. ________ just a few pictures.

7. **A.** Did you buy any clothing?
   B. No, ____________.
   A. What ______________________?
   B. ____________________ souvenirs.

8. **A.** Did you swim in the Mediterranean?
   B. No, ____________.
   A. Where ______________________?
   B. _________ in the pool at our hotel.

9. **A.** Did you see the Colosseum?
   B. No, ____________.
   A. What ______________________?
   B. __________________ the Vatican.

10. **A.** Did you get around the city by taxi?
    B. No, ____________.
    A. How ________________________?
    B. ______________________ by bus.

11. **A.** Did you meet a lot of Italians?
    B. No, ____________.
    A. Who ________________________?
    B. __________ a lot of other tourists.

12. **A.** Did you come home by plane?
    B. No, ____________.
    A. How ________________________?
    B. _____________________ by boat.

Write in your journal about a trip you took. Where did you go? How did you get there? Where did you stay? What did you do there? How long were you there? Did you have a good time?

(If you have some photographs of your trip, bring them to class and talk about them with other students.)

PRONUNCIATION *Did you*

Listen. Then say it.

Did you go to Madrid?

Did you speak Spanish?

Where did you stay?

What did you do?

Say it. Then listen.

Did you meet a lot of people?

Did you have a good time?

How did you get there?

When did you get home?

GRAMMAR FOCUS

Simple Past Tense

What did	I he she it we you they	do?

I He She It We You They	worked.

Did	I he she it we you they	fall asleep?

Yes,	I he she it we you they	did.

No,	I he she it we you they	didn't.

I He She It	was	tired.
We You They	were	

I He She It	wasn't	tired.
We You They	weren't	

Past Continuous Tense

I He She It	was	working.
We You They	were	

Choose the correct answer.

1. A. What (do you did did you do) last weekend?
   B. We (went were going) to the beach.
2. A. Did you (ate eat) all your dinner?
   B. No, we (did didn't). We (wasn't weren't) very hungry.
3. A. How (did they burn they burned) themselves?
   B. They (were baking were baked) cookies.
4. A. Did you (sleep slept) well last night?
   B. Yes, I (did didn't). I (were was) very tired.
5. A. (Did he took Did he take) the bus?
   B. No, he (wasn't didn't). He (take took) the train.
6. A. (How How did) your grandmother (fall fell)?
   B. She (was falling fell) while (was she she was) getting off a bus.

3

Review:
Future: Going to
Future: Will
Future Continuous Tense

Time Expressions
Possessive Pronouns

- Describing Future Plans and Intentions
- Telling About the Future
- Expressing Time and Duration
- Talking on the Telephone
- Plans for the Future
- Asking a Favor

Vocabulary Preview

yesterday — *today* — *tomorrow*

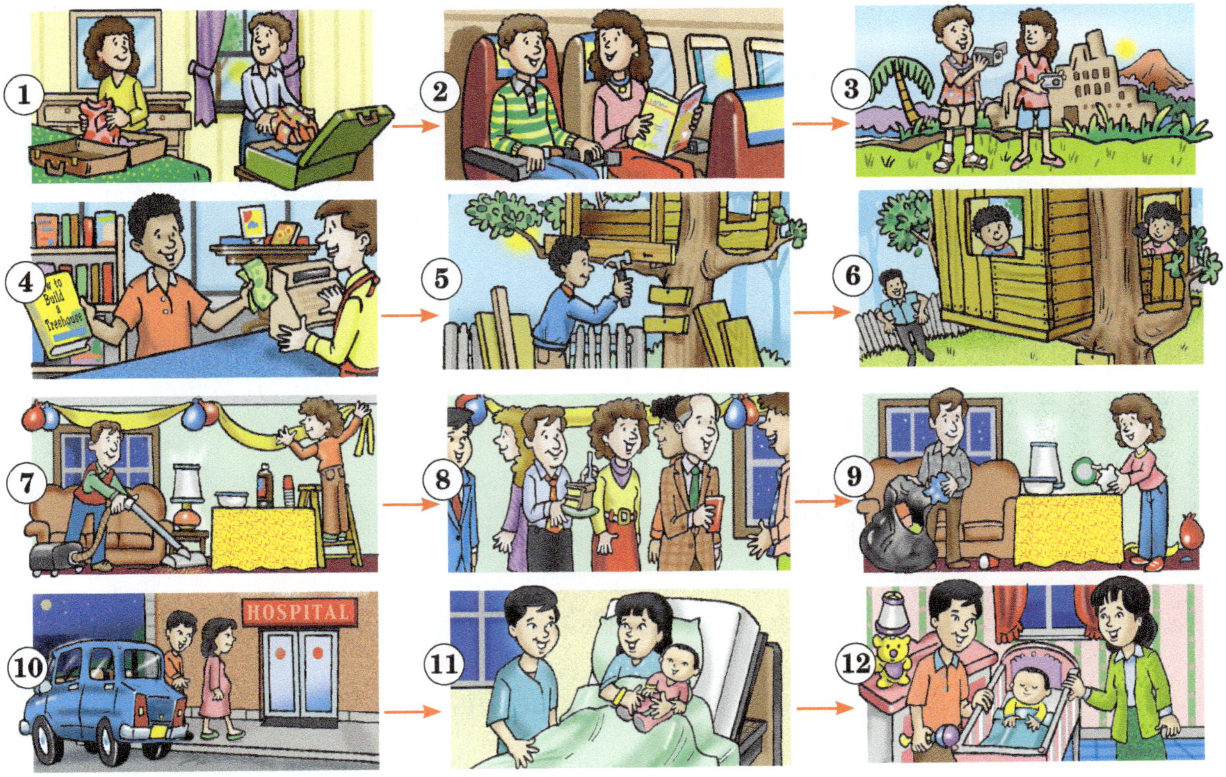

1. yesterday morning
2. this morning
3. tomorrow morning
4. yesterday afternoon
5. this afternoon
6. tomorrow afternoon
7. yesterday evening
8. this evening
9. tomorrow evening
10. last night
11. tonight
12. tomorrow night

What Are They Going to Do?

What	am	I	going to do?
	is	he / she / it	
	are	we / you / they	

(I am)	I'm	going to read.
(He is)	He's	
(She is)	She's	
(It is)	It's	
(We are)	We're	
(You are)	You're	
(They are)	They're	

Time Expressions

yesterday / this / tomorrow	morning / afternoon / evening	last night / tonight / tomorrow night
last / this / next	week / month / year / Sunday / Monday / . . . spring / summer / . . . January / February / . . .	

A. Are you going to buy a donut this morning?

B. No, I'm not. I bought a donut YESTERDAY morning.

A. What are you going to buy?

B. I'm going to buy a muffin.

1. Is Mr. Hopper going to have cake for dessert tonight?
ice cream

2. Is Valerie going to sing folk songs this evening?
Broadway show tunes

3. Are you and your family going to go to Europe this summer?
Hawaii

4. Is Gary going to wear his gray suit today?
his blue suit

5. Are your parents going to watch the movie on Channel 4 this Friday night?
the news program on Channel 7

6. Is Elizabeth going to go out with Jonathan this Saturday evening?
Bob

7. Is the chef going to make onion soup today?
pea soup

8. Is your sister going to take biology this semester?
astronomy

9. Are you and your brother going to play cards this afternoon?
chess

10. Are you going to be Superman this Halloween?
Batman

READING

PLANS FOR THE WEEKEND

It's Friday afternoon, and all the employees at the Liberty Insurance Company are thinking about their plans for the weekend. Milton is going to work in his garden. Diane is going to go hiking in the mountains. Carmen and Tom are going to play tennis. Jack is going to go water-skiing. Kate is going to build a tree house for her children. And Ray and his family are going to have a picnic.

Unfortunately, the employees at the Liberty Insurance Company are going to be very disappointed. According to the radio, it's going to "rain cats and dogs" all weekend.

✓ READING *CHECK-UP*

Q & A

The employees at the Liberty Insurance Company are talking with each other. Using this model, create dialogs based on the story.

A. Tell me, *Milton*, what are you going to do this weekend?
B. I'm going to *work in my garden*. How about you, *Diane*? What are YOU going to do?
A. I'm going to *go hiking in the mountains*.
B. Well, have a nice weekend.
A. You, too.

How About You?

What are you going to do this weekend? What's the weather forecast?

LISTENING

Listen to the conversation and choose the answer that is true.

1. a. He's going to wear his gray suit.
   b. He's going to wear his brown suit.
2. a. They're going to have dinner at home.
   b. They're going to have dinner at a restaurant.
3. a. They're going to watch Channel 5.
   b. They're going to watch Channel 9.
4. a. He's going to call a mechanic.
   b. He's going to call an electrician.
5. a. She's going to go to the supermarket tomorrow.
   b. She's going to work in her garden tomorrow.
6. a. They're going to buy the computer.
   b. They aren't going to buy the computer.

Will Ms. Martinez Return Soon?

(I will)	I'll	work.
(He will)	He'll	
(She will)	She'll	
(It will)	It'll	
(We will)	We'll	
(You will)	You'll	
(They will)	They'll	

I	won't work. (will not)
He	
She	
It	
We	
You	
They	

A. Will Ms. Martinez return soon?

B. Yes, she will. She'll return in a little while.

A. Will your sister return soon?

B. No, she won't. She won't return for a long time.

1. Will the play begin soon?
   Yes, ________. ________ *at 7:30.*

2. Will the concert begin soon?
   No, ________. ________ *until 8:00.*

3. Will Ken and Kim see each other again soon?
   Yes, ________. ________ *this Saturday night.*

4. Will Larry and Lisa see each other again soon?
   No, ________. ________ *until next year.*

5. Will the train arrive soon?
   Yes, ________. ________ *in a few minutes.*

6. Will Flight 216 arrive soon?
   No, ________. ________ *for several hours.*

7. Will David get out of the hospital soon?
   Yes, ________. ________ *in a few days.*

8. Will Ralph get out of jail soon?
   No, ________. ________ *for a few years.*

Will You Be Home This Evening?

I'll He'll She'll It'll We'll You'll They'll	be working.

A. Will you be home this evening?

B. Yes, I will. I'll be **watching videos**.

A. Will Nancy be home this evening?

B. No, she won't. She'll be **working overtime**.

1. *you*
   pay bills

2. *Angela*
   shop at the mall

3. *Mr. and Mrs. Chen*
   paint their kitchen

4. *your sister*
   attend a meeting

5. *you and your family*
   ice skate

6. *Vincent*
   browse the web

7. *you*
   do research at the library

8. *Tess*
   fill out her income tax form

9. *Mr. and Mrs. Silva*
   work out at their health club

Can You Call Back a Little Later?

Create conversations based on the model above.

1. *do homework*

2. *iron*

3. *wash my windows*

4. *have dinner*

5. *give the kids a bath*

6.

Could You Do Me a Favor?

I	me	mine
he	him	his
she	her	hers
it	it	—
we	us	ours
you	you	yours
they	them	theirs

A. Could you do me a favor?

B. Sure. What is it?

A. I have to fix a flat tire, and I don't have a jack. Could I possibly borrow yours?

B. I'm sorry. I'm afraid I don't have one.

A. Oh. Do you know anybody who does?

B. Yes. You should call Joe. I'm sure he'll be happy to lend you his.

A. Thanks. I'll call him right away.

A. Could you do me a favor?

B. Sure. What is it?

A. I have to ________, and I don't have a ________. Could I possibly borrow yours?

B. I'm sorry. I'm afraid I don't have one.

A. Oh. Do you know anybody who does?

B. Yes. You should call ________. I'm sure ______'ll be happy to lend you ______ (his/hers/theirs).

A. Thanks. I'll call ______ (him/her/them) right away.

1. *fix my front steps*
   hammer

2. *assemble my new bookshelf*
   screwdriver

3. *write a composition*
   dictionary

4. *adjust my satellite dish*
   ladder

5. *go to a wedding*
   tuxedo

6.

How to Say It!

Asking for a Favor

A. Could you do me a favor?
Could you possibly do me a favor?
Could you do a favor for me?
Could I ask you a favor?

B. Sure. What is it?

Practice the conversations in this lesson again. Ask for a favor in different ways.

READING

SAYING GOOD-BYE

Mr. and Mrs. Karpov are at the Moscow airport. They're saying good-bye to their son Sasha and his family. It's a very emotional day. In a few minutes, Sasha and his family will get on a plane and fly to Canada. They won't be coming back. They're leaving Russia permanently, and Mr. and Mrs. Karpov won't be seeing them for a long, long time.

Sasha and his family are excited about their plans for the future. They're going to stay with his wife's relatives in Toronto. Sasha will work in the family's restaurant. His wife, Marina, will take any job she can find during the day, and she'll study English at night. The children will begin school in September.

Mr. and Mrs. Karpov are both happy and sad. They're happy because they know that their son will have a good life in his new home. However, they're sad because they know they're going to be very lonely. Their apartment will be quiet and empty, and they won't see their grandchildren grow up.

Some day Mr. and Mrs. Karpov will visit Toronto, or perhaps they'll even move there. But until then, they're going to miss their family very much. As you can imagine, it's very difficult for them to say good-bye.

READING *CHECK-UP*

TRUE OR FALSE?

1. Sasha and his family will be leaving Russia for a few minutes.
2. Marina's relatives live in Toronto.
3. Mr. Karpov is happy, and Mrs. Karpov is sad.
4. Mr. and Mrs. Karpov might move to Toronto.
5. Mr. and Mrs. Karpov are sad because they'll be at the Moscow airport until they visit Toronto or move there.

How About You?

- Tell about an emotional day in your life when you had to say good-bye.
- Tell about YOUR plans for the future.

ON YOUR OWN *Looking Forward*

Jerry is looking forward to this weekend. He isn't going to think about work. He's going to read a few magazines, work on his car, and relax at home with his family.

Amanda is looking forward to her birthday. Her sister is going to have a party for her, and all her co-workers and friends are going to be there.

Mr. and Mrs. Cook are looking forward to their summer vacation. They're going to go camping. They're going to hike several miles every day, take a lot of pictures, and forget about all their problems at home.

Mr. and Mrs. Lee are looking forward to their retirement. They're going to get up late every morning, visit friends every afternoon, and enjoy quiet evenings at home together.

What are YOU looking forward to? A birthday? a holiday? a day off? Talk about it with other students in your class.

Write in your journal about something you're looking forward to: What are you looking forward to? When is it going to happen? What are you going to do?

PRONUNCIATION *Going to*

going to = gonna

Listen. Then say it.

Are you going to buy bread today?

What are you going to eat?

I'm going to go camping.

Say it. Then listen.

Is she going to watch TV?

What's he going to wear?

They're going to make dinner.

GRAMMAR FOCUS

Future: Going to

What	am	I	going to do?
	is	he she it	
	are	we you they	

(I am)	I'm	going to read.
(He is) (She is) (It is)	He's She's It's	
(We are) (You are) (They are)	We're You're They're	

Possessive Pronouns

mine
his
hers
—
ours
yours
theirs

Future: Will

(I will) (He will) (She will) (It will) (We will) (You will) (They will)	I'll He'll She'll It'll We'll You'll They'll	work.

I He She It We You They	won't work.

Future Continuous Tense

(I will) (He will) (She will) (It will) (We will) (You will) (They will)	I'll He'll She'll It'll We'll You'll They'll	be working.

Complete the sentences.

1. A. What _____ you _____ _____ buy?
   B. _____ _____ _____ buy a new suit.
2. A. _____ Ms. Romero be back soon?
   B. Yes, _____ _____. _____ _____ back in an hour.
3. A. I don't have a ladder. Can I possibly borrow yours?
   B. I can't find _____. You should ask Mr. King. I'm sure _____ be happy to lend you _____.
4. A. Are you and your wife _____ _____ go to Canada for your vacation?
   B. No. I think _____ probably _____ to Mexico.
5. A. _____ the flight from Dallas arrive soon?
   B. No, _____ _____. _____ _____ _____ until after midnight.
6. A. _____ your parents be home this evening?
   B. Yes, _____ _____. _____ _____ watching their favorite TV program.

Feature Article
Fact File
Around the World
Interview
We've Got Mail!

SIDE by SIDE Gazette

Global Exchange
Listening
Fun with Idioms
What Are They Saying?

Volume 3 Number 1

Immigration Around the World

Where do immigrants move, and why?

More than 145 million immigrants live outside their native countries. Immigrants move to other countries for different reasons. Some people move because of war, political or economic problems, or natural disasters such as earthquakes and floods. Some immigrants move to be with family members, to marry, or to find better living conditions.

Where are immigrants moving from? And what countries are they moving to? One of the largest immigration flows is from Latin America and Asia to the United States. Another immigrant flow is from Eastern Europe, the former Soviet republics, and North Africa to Western Europe. Many immigrants also move from Africa and Asia to the Middle East. In countries such as Saudi Arabia, 90% of the total population is now foreign born.

When immigrants arrive in a new country, they often live in urban neighborhoods. As a result of immigration, many city neighborhoods change. Immigrants open new stores, restaurants, and other businesses. For example, the historic Esquilino neighborhood in Rome is now the home of a large number of Chinese immigrants. There are also many new immigrants from Albania, Moldova, Bulgaria, and Ukraine. In some schools in Athens, 50% of the children are foreign born. Los Angeles and New York are two cities in the United States with very large immigrant populations. In Los Angeles, 37% of the population is foreign born, and children in the public schools speak 82 different languages. In New York, 40% of the population is foreign born, and children speak 140 different languages in the schools.

Immigrants arriving in their new country

Ellis Island

Ellis Island was an immigration center on an island in the harbor of New York City. Between 1892 and 1954, 12 million immigrants passed through Ellis Island. At Ellis Island, immigration officials checked immigrants' documents, gave them medical examinations, and decided if the immigrants could stay in the United States. Most immigrants came from Italy, Russia, Hungary, Austria, Austria-Hungary, Germany, England, and Ireland. More than 40% of all Americans today have a present or past relative who came through Ellis Island.

Ellis Island registration hall

FACT FILE

Countries with Large Numbers of Immigrants

Country	Immigrant Population (in millions)
United States	28.4
Germany	7.5
Saudi Arabia	6
Canada	4.9
Australia	4.4
France	4.3

Around the World

Immigrant Neighborhoods

There are many interesting immigrant neighborhoods around the world. In these neighborhoods, immigrants can often speak their native languages, buy products from their countries, and eat in restaurants that serve their favorite foods.

a Cuban neighborhood in Miami, Florida

Vietnamese immigrants in Sydney, Australia

Turkish immigrants in Berlin, Germany

Chinatown in Toronto, Canada

Japanese immigrants in Sao Paulo, Brazil

a Russian neighborhood in Brooklyn, New York

What are different immigrant neighborhoods you know?

Interview

A Side by Side Gazette reporter recently visited Mr. Tran Nguyen, a Vietnamese immigrant in Australia. Mr. Nguyen lives and works in a Vietnamese and Chinese neighborhood in the suburbs of Melbourne.

Q: When did you immigrate to Australia, and why?

A: Well, my brother left Vietnam in 1983 and came here to Australia. Seven years later, his wife and children joined him. I came here three years ago with my wife and children to be with my brother and his family.

Q: Do you work?

A: Yes. I work seven days a week in my brother's restaurant, and I go to English classes at night.

Q: What did you do in Vietnam?

A: I was a teacher. I taught mathematics. I want to be a teacher here someday, but first I want to send my children to college.

Q: What do you miss most about Vietnam?

A: I miss my community and my friends. In Vietnam, people took care of each other. It's not the same here. Everyone here works very hard. People are very busy. They don't have much time to spend with friends.

Q: What do you like about your life here?

A: We have many opportunities. My wife and I both have good jobs, and my son and daughter will go to college someday. I think we will have a very good future here, and we're very grateful.

We've Got Mail!

Dear Side by Side,

I have a question about tenses in English. Sometimes I hear people use the present tense when they are talking about the future. For example, I was watching a TV program in English yesterday, and I heard a man say, "I'm flying to London tomorrow. My plane leaves at 9:30." But if a man is talking about tomorrow, shouldn't he use the future tense? I think the correct way to say this is: "I'm going to fly to London tomorrow. My plane will leave at 9:30." Did the man on the TV program make a mistake?

Sincerely,
"Tense About the Future"

Dear "Tense About the Future,"

Your question is a very good one. No, the man on the TV program didn't make a mistake. We often use the present tense to talk about events in the future or about definite plans that we have. For example, you can say:

My brother's wedding is next Saturday.
I'm having a party tomorrow.
They're going to the beach this weekend.
The plumber is coming tomorrow morning.

We can also use the present tense to talk about future events that happen at a definite time or on a regular schedule. For example, you can say:

The movie begins at 7:30 tonight.
The office opens tomorrow morning at 9 A.M.
The train arrives at 6:15.
The store closes tonight at 10 P.M.

So, you don't need to be "tense" about the future! You can use both the present and the future tenses to talk about future time.

We hope this answers your question. Thanks for your letter, and good luck with your English!

Sincerely,
Side by Side

Global Exchange

NickyG: Hi. It's Sunday night here, and I just finished my biology homework. Before I turn off my computer, I want to tell you about my weekend. It was really great. I went camping with some of my friends. We left early Saturday morning and drove to the mountains. We hiked for several hours to a beautiful lake. We went swimming, we cooked over a campfire, and we slept outside. We told stories and sang songs until after midnight. In the morning, we made a big breakfast, we swam again, and then we packed up our things, hiked back to the car, and came home. How about you? How was your weekend? Write back soon. Okay?

Smile9: Hi. It's Monday morning here. I'm sitting in the computer lab at my school, and your message just arrived! I'm happy to hear from you again. My weekend wasn't as exciting as yours. I have final exams in all my courses this week, so I stayed home and studied all weekend. But I'm really looking forward to next weekend. Our family is going to travel to the place where my parents grew up. We're having a big family reunion on Saturday. All my relatives will be there. We don't see them very often, so it will be a very special time. I'll tell you about it when I return. Oh. Here comes my teacher! I've got to go! Talk to you soon.

Send a message to a keypal. Tell about what you did last weekend. Tell about your plans for next weekend.

LISTENING

You Have Five Messages!

e	1	Sarah	a.	will be visiting his parents.
____	2	Bob	b.	will be studying.
____	3	Paula	c.	will be attending a wedding.
____	4	Joe	d.	will go to the party.
____	5	Carla	e.	will be taking her uncle to the hospital.

FUN with IDIOMS

Do You Know These Expressions?

_e_	1.	It's raining cats and dogs!	a.	I'll call you.
____	2.	What's cooking?	b.	It was difficult.
____	3.	I'm tied up right now.	c.	It was easy.
____	4.	I'll give you a ring tomorrow.	d.	What's new?
____	5.	The English test was a piece of cake!	e.	It's raining very hard.
____	6.	The English test was no picnic!	f.	I'm busy.

What Are They Saying?

4

Present Perfect Tense

- **Describing Actions That Have Occurred**
- **Describing Actions That Haven't Occurred Yet**
- **Making Recommendations**
- **Things to Do Where You Live**
- **Making Lists**

VOCABULARY PREVIEW

Things to Do Today

1 
☐ go to the bank

2 
☐ do the laundry

3 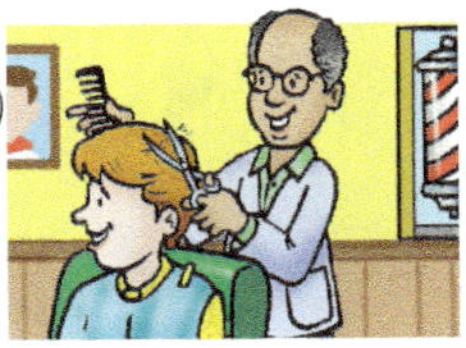
☐ get a haircut

4 
☐ write to Grandma

5 
☐ take the dog for a walk

6 
☐ give the dog a bath

7 
☐ speak to the landlord

8 
☐ drive the kids to their dance lesson

9 
☐ eat lunch

10 
☐ ride my exercise bike

11 
☐ swim

12 
☐ see a movie

Things I've Done Today: I've . . .

☑ **1.** gone to the bank
☑ **2.** done the laundry
☑ **3.** gotten a haircut
☑ **4.** written to Grandma
☑ **5.** taken the dog for a walk
☑ **6.** given the dog a bath
☑ **7.** spoken to the landlord
☑ **8.** driven the kids to their dance lesson
☑ **9.** eaten lunch
☑ **10.** ridden my exercise bike
☑ **11.** swum
☑ **12.** seen a movie

I've Driven Trucks for Many Years

A. Do you know how to **drive** trucks?

B. Yes. I've **driven** trucks for many years.

1. *write reports*
   written

2. *fly airplanes*
   flown

3. *take X-rays*
   taken

4. *speak Swahili*
   spoken

5. *eat with chopsticks*
   eaten

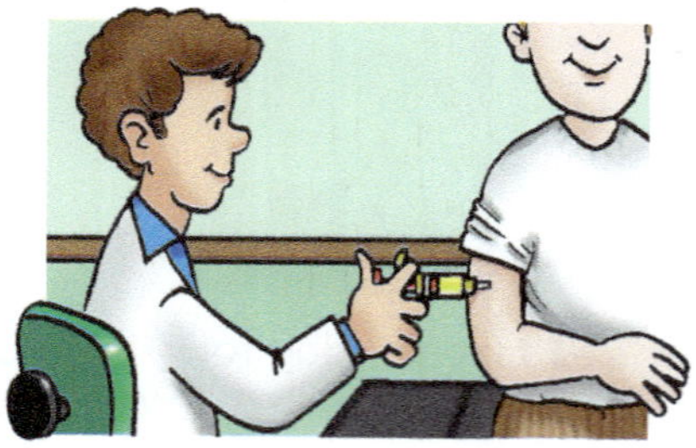

6. *give injections*
   given

7. *draw cartoons*
   drawn

8. *do yoga*
   done

9. *ride horses*
   ridden

I've Never Eaten Lunch with the Boss

A. I'm going to **eat** lunch with the boss tomorrow.

B. I'm jealous. I've never **eaten** lunch with the boss.

1. *fly in a helicopter*
flown

2. *see a Broadway show*
seen

3. *go on a cruise*
gone

4. *sing at the White House*
sung

5. *swim at the Ritz Hotel*
swum

6. *get a raise*
gotten

7. *be on television*
been

8. *take a ride in a hot-air balloon*
taken

9. *ride in a limousine*
ridden

Have You Ever Seen a Rainbow?

see
saw
seen

A. Have you ever **seen** a rainbow?

B. Yes, I have. I **saw** a rainbow last year.

go
went
gone

1. *go scuba diving*

give
gave
given

2. *give a speech*

wear
wore
worn

3. *wear a kimono*

eat
ate
eaten

4. *eat cotton candy*

take
took
taken

5. *take a first-aid course*

fall
fell
fallen

6. *fall asleep in class*

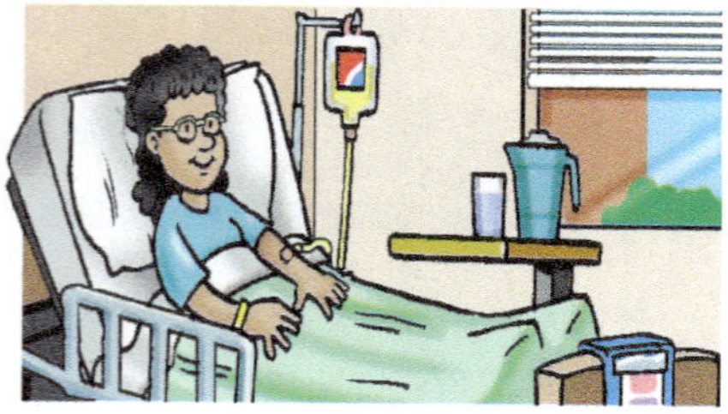

be
was
been

7. *be in the hospital*

get
got
gotten

8. *get stuck in an elevator*

Have You Written the Report Yet?

Have { I / we / you / they } eaten?
Has { he / she / it }

Yes, { I / we / you / they } have.
{ he / she / it } has.

write
wrote
written

A. Have you **written** the report yet?

B. Yes, I have. I **wrote** the report a little while ago.

go
went
gone

A. Has David **gone** to the bank yet?

B. Yes, he has. He **went** to the bank a little while ago.

drive
drove
driven

1. *you*
drive the new van

give
gave
given

2. *Nancy*
give her presentation

get
got
gotten

3. *the employees*
get their paychecks

take
took
taken

4. *you and Robert*
take inventory

meet
met
met

5. *George*
meet the new boss

explain
explained
explained

6. *I*
explain the present perfect tense

He's Already Gone Bowling This Week

(I have)	I've	eaten.
(We have)	We've	
(You have)	You've	
(They have)	They've	
(He has)	He's	
(She has)	She's	
(It has)	It's	

go
went
gone

A. Why isn't Charlie going to **go** bowling tonight?

B. He's already **gone** bowling this week.

A. Really? When?

B. He **went** bowling yesterday.

see
saw
seen

1. Why isn't Vicky going to see a movie this evening?

eat
ate
eaten

2. Why aren't Mr. and Mrs. Kendall going to eat at a restaurant tonight?

get
got
gotten

3. Why isn't Roy going to get a haircut today?

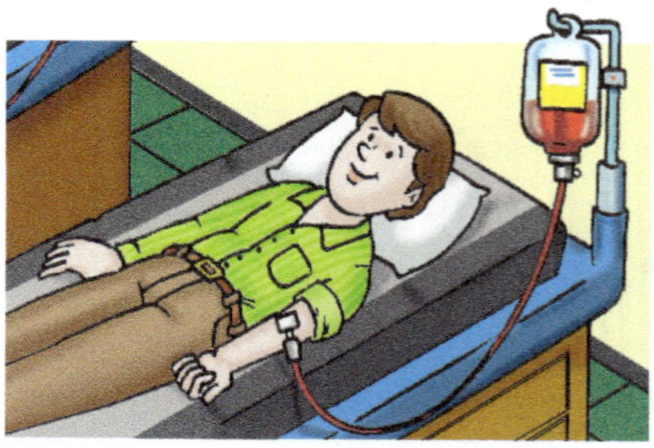

give
gave
given

4. Why aren't you going to give blood today?

take
took
taken

5. Why isn't Shirley going to take her children to the zoo this afternoon?

wear
wore
worn

6. Why isn't Fred going to wear his purple tie today?

drive
drove
driven

7. Why aren't you and your family going to drive to the mountains today?

write
wrote
written

8. Why isn't Julie going to write to her best friend today?

do
did
done

9. Why isn't Gary going to do his laundry today?

swim
swam
swum

10. Why aren't your parents going to swim at the health club today?

buy
bought
bought

11. Why aren't you going to buy bananas today?

have
had
had

12. Why aren't Mr. and Mrs. Davis going to have spaghetti for dinner tonight?

wash
washed
washed

13. Why isn't Jim going to wash his car this morning?

play
played
played

14. Why isn't your grandmother going to play Bingo today?

READING

WE CAN'T DECIDE

My friends and I can't decide what to do tonight. I don't want to see a movie. I've already seen a movie this week. Maggie doesn't want to go bowling. She has already gone bowling this week. Mark doesn't want to eat at a restaurant. He has already eaten at a restaurant this week. Betty and Mike don't want to play cards. They have already played cards this week. And NOBODY wants to go dancing. We have all gone dancing this week.

It's already 9 P.M., and we still haven't decided what we're going to do tonight.

ROLE PLAY

You and other students are the people in the story above. Create a role play based on the situation. Use these lines to start your conversation.

A. Look! It's already 9 P.M., and we still haven't decided what we're going to do tonight. Does anybody have any ideas?
B. I don't know.
C. Do you want to see a movie?
D. No, not me. I've already . . .
E. Does anybody want to . . . ?
F. I don't. I've already . . .
G. I have an idea. Let's . . .
H. No, I don't want to do that. I've already . . .

COMPLETE THE STORY

Fill in the correct words to complete the story.

Alvin has a very bad cold. He has been sick all week. He has tried very hard to get rid of his cold, but nothing he has done has helped. At the beginning of the week, he went to a clinic and saw a doctor. He followed the doctor's advice all week. He stayed home, took aspirin, drank* orange juice, ate chicken soup, and rested in bed.

At this point, Alvin is extremely frustrated. Even though he has ________ 1 to a clinic and ________ 2 a doctor, ________ 3 home, ________ 4 aspirin, ________ 5 orange juice, ________ 6 chicken soup, and ________ 7 in bed, he STILL has a very bad cold. Nothing he has ________ 8 has helped.

* drink – drank – drunk

They Haven't Had the Time

I / We / You / They } haven't (have not) eaten.*

He / She / It } hasn't (has not) eaten.*

A. Do you like to **swim**?

B. Yes, but I haven't **swum** in a long time.

A. Why not?

B. I haven't had the time.

A. Does Rita like to **draw**?

B. Yes, but she hasn't **drawn** in a long time.

A. Why not?

B. She hasn't had the time.

1. Do you like to ride your bicycle?

2. Does Arthur like to write poetry?

3. Does Kathy like to go kayaking?

4. Do you and your brother like to play Monopoly?

5. Does Laura like to make her own clothes?

6. Do you like to see your old friends?

7. Do Mr. and Mrs. Bell like to take dance lessons?

8. Does Grandpa like to do magic tricks?

9.

* In the present perfect tense, the word after **have** or **has** is a past participle. Some past participles are the same as the past tense (for example, **played**, **washed**, **made**). Other past participles are different from the past tense (for example, **swum**, **drawn**, **ridden**). We will tell you when the past participles are different. A list of these words is in the Appendix at the end of the book.

Has Timmy Gone to Bed Yet?

Have	I we you they	eaten?
Has	he she it	

No,	I we you they	haven't.
	he she it	hasn't.

A. Has Timmy gone to bed yet?

B. No, he hasn't. He has to go to bed now.

1. *Amanda*
do her homework

2. *you*
take your medicine

3. *James*
get up

4. *Debbie and Danny*
leave for school

5. *Jennifer*
call her supervisor

6. *you*
write your term paper

7. *you and your sister*
feed the dog

8. *you*
speak to your landlord

9. *Harry*
pay his electric bill

READING

WORKING OVERTIME

I'm an employee of the Goodwell Computer Company. This is a typical Friday afternoon at our office. All the employees are working overtime. We haven't gone home because we haven't finished our work yet. Friday is always a very busy day.

The secretary still hasn't typed two important letters. The bookkeeper hasn't written all the paychecks. The office clerks haven't delivered all the mail. And the boss still hasn't spoken to three important people who are waiting to see her.

As for me, I'm the custodian, and I haven't finished my work yet either. I still haven't cleaned all the offices because my co-workers haven't gone home yet! I'm not really surprised. Friday is always a very busy day at our office.

✓ READING *CHECK-UP*

Q & A

The custodian at the Goodwell Computer Company is talking with the employees on a typical Friday afternoon. Using this model, create dialogs based on the story.

A. I see you haven't gone home yet.
B. No, I haven't. I still haven't *typed two important letters*.
A. Well, have a good weekend.
B. You, too.

WHAT'S THE WORD?

1. A. Have you (see) ______ the letter from the Lexon Company?
B. Yes. I ______ it on your desk.

2. A. Have you (eat) ______ lunch yet?
B. Yes. I ______ a few minutes ago.

3. A. Has the bookkeeper (go) ______ to the bank yet?
B. Yes, she ______. She ______ there this morning.

4. A. Have you (speak) ______ to the boss about your vacation?
B. Yes, I ______. I ______ to her about it yesterday.

5. A. Have you (make) ______ plans for my trip to Chicago yet?
B. Yes. I ______ them yesterday.

6. A. Has anybody (read) ______ today's *New York Times*?
B. Yes. I ______ it on my way to work.

7. A. Has the office clerk (take) ______ the mail to the post office yet?
B. No, he ______. He ______ it to the mail room, but ______ ______ ______ it to the post office yet.

8. A. Has John (finish) ______ his work?
B. Yes, he ______. He's already (go) ______ home.

Have You Seen Any Good Movies Recently?

A. Have you seen any good movies recently?

B. Yes, I have. I saw a very good movie last week.

A. Really? What movie did you see?

B. I saw *The Wedding Dancer*.

A. Oh. How was it?

B. It was excellent. It's one of the best movies I've ever seen.

A. Have you __________ any good __________s recently?

B. Yes, I have. I __________ a very good __________ last week.

A. Really? What __________ did you __________?

B. I __________ "______________________________."

A. Oh. How was it?

B. It was excellent. It's one of the best __________s I've ever __________.

1. *read • book*

2. *rent • video*

3. *go to • restaurant*

How to Say It!

Expressing Satisfaction

A. How was it?

B. It was excellent.
It was very good.
It was wonderful.
It was great.
It was fantastic.
It was terrific.
It was phenomenal.
It was awesome.

Practice the conversations in this lesson again. Express satisfaction in different ways.

READING

LINDA LIKES NEW YORK

Linda has lived in New York for a long time. She has done a lot of things in New York. She has gone to the top of the Empire State Building, she has visited the Statue of Liberty, she has taken a tour of the United Nations, and she has seen several Broadway shows.

However, there are a lot of things she hasn't done yet. She hasn't gone to any museums, she hasn't seen Ellis Island, and she hasn't been in Times Square on New Year's Eve.

Linda likes New York. She has done a lot of things, and there are still a lot more things to do.

LISTENING

Linda is on vacation in San Francisco. This is her list of things to do. Check the things on the list Linda has already done.

- ___ see the Golden Gate Bridge
- ___ visit Golden Gate Park
- ___ take a tour of Alcatraz prison
- ___ go to Chinatown
- ___ ride a cable car
- ___ eat at Fisherman's Wharf
- ___ buy souvenirs

Alan is a secretary in a very busy office. This is his list of things to do before 5 P.M. on Friday. Check the things on the list Alan has already done.

- ___ call Mrs. Porter
- ___ type the letter to the Mervis Company
- ___ take the mail to the post office
- ___ go to the bank
- ___ send an e-mail to the company's office in Denver
- ___ speak to the boss about my salary

It's Saturday, and Judy and Paul Johnson are doing lots of things around the house. This is the list of things they have to do today. Check the things on the list they've already done.

- ___ do the laundry
- ___ wash the kitchen windows
- ___ pay the bills
- ___ give the dog a bath
- ___ clean the garage
- ___ fix the bathroom sink
- ___ repair the fence
- ___ vacuum the living room rug

Make a list of things you usually do at school, at work, or at home. Then check the things you've already done this week. Share your list with other students. Tell about what you've done and what you haven't done.

PRONUNCIATION Contractions with *is* & *has*

he is = he's he has = he's	she is = she's she has = she's

Listen. Then say it.

He is a good painter.

He has painted for a long time.

She is a good teacher.

She has taught for a long time.

Say it. Then listen.

He is a taxi driver.

He has driven a taxi for a long time.

She is an actress.

She has acted for a long time.

Think about your experiences in the place where you live. What have you done? What haven't you done yet? Write about it in your journal.

GRAMMAR FOCUS

Present Perfect Tense

(I have) (We have) (You have) (They have)	I've We've You've They've	eaten.
(He has) (She has) (It has)	He's She's It's	

I We You They	haven't	eaten.
He She It	hasn't	

Have	I we you they	eaten?
Has	he she it	

Yes,	I we you they	have.
	he she it	has.

No,	I we you they	haven't.
	he she it	hasn't.

Irregular Verbs

be – was/were – been
do – did – done
draw – drew – drawn
drink – drank – drunk
drive – drove – driven
eat – ate – eaten
fall – fell – fallen
fly – flew – flown
get – got – gotten
give – gave – given
go – went – gone
ride – rode – ridden
see – saw – seen
sing – sang – sung
speak – spoke – spoken
swim – swam – swum
take – took – taken
wear – wore – worn
write – wrote – written

Complete the sentences with the correct forms of these verbs.

be	draw	go	ride	see	sing	take	wear

1. I love to draw. _____ _____ for many years.
2. _____ you ever _____ a rainbow?
3. My parents _____ never _____ dance lessons.
4. _____ already _____ that song. We _____ it a little while ago.
5. My grandson _____ _____ his bicycle in a long time.
6. _____ you ever _____ on TV? Yes, I _____.
7. Joe _____ already _____ that tie this week. He _____ it yesterday.
8. _____ Marta _____ to sleep yet? Yes, _____ _____. She _____ to sleep an hour ago.

5

Present Perfect vs. Present Tense
Present Perfect vs. Past Tense
Since / For

- Discussing Duration of Activity
- Medical Symptoms and Problems
- Career Advancement
- Telling About Family Members

Vocabulary Preview

1. astronaut
2. cashier
3. clerk
4. computer programmer
5. doctor/physician
6. guidance counselor
7. guitarist
8. journalist
9. manager
10. musician
11. police officer
12. president
13. salesperson
14. taxi driver
15. vice president

How Long?

for	since
three hours	three o'clock
two days	yesterday afternoon
a week	last week
a long time	2000
.	.
.	.
.	.

A. How long have you known* each other?

B. We've known each other **for three years**.

*know – knew – known

A. How long have you been sick?

B. I've been sick **since last Friday**.

1. How long have Tom and Janet known each other?
two years

2. How long have Mr. and Mrs. Garcia been married?
1995

3. How long have you had a stomachache?
ten o'clock this morning

4. How long has Melanie had the measles?
five days

5. How long has Ms. Bennett been a guidance counselor?
nineteen years

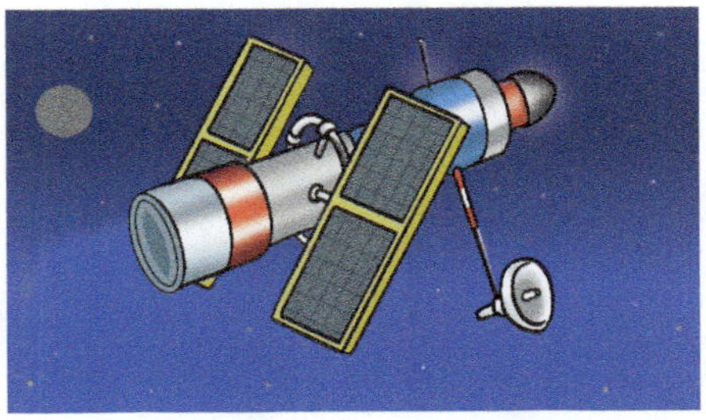

6. How long have there been satellites in space?
1957

7. How long have you owned this car?
three and a half years

8. How long has Bob owned his own house?
1999

9. How long have you been interested in astronomy?
many years

10. How long has Glen been interested in photography?
a long time

11. How long have you been here?
1979

12. How long has your son had blue hair?
a week

READING

A VERY DEDICATED DOCTOR

Dr. Fernando's waiting room is very full today. A lot of people are waiting to see him, and they're hoping that the doctor can help them. George's neck has been stiff for more than a week. Martha has had a bad headache since yesterday, and Lenny has felt dizzy since early this morning. Carol has had a high fever for two days, Bob's knee has been swollen for three weeks, Bill's arm has been black and blue since last weekend, and Tommy and Julie have had little red spots all over their bodies for the past twenty-four hours.

Dr. Fernando has been in the office since early this morning. He has already seen a lot of patients, and he will certainly see many more before the day is over. Dr. Fernando's patients don't know it, but he also isn't feeling well. He has had a pain in his back since last Thursday, but he hasn't taken any time to stay at home and rest. He has had a lot of patients this week, and he's a very dedicated doctor.

READING *CHECK-UP*

Q & A

Dr. Fernando's patients are talking to him about their problems. Using this model, create dialogs based on the story.

A. So how are you feeling today, *George*?
B. Not very well, Dr. Fernando.
A. What seems to be the problem?
B. *My neck is stiff.*
A. I see. Tell me, how long *has your neck been stiff?*
B. *For more than a week.*

CHOOSE

1. They've known each other since _____.
   a. 2000
   b. three years

2. I've been interested in astronomy for _____.
   a. last year
   b. one year

3. She has been a doctor for _____.
   a. two years ago
   b. two years

4. He has had a toothache since _____.
   a. yesterday
   b. two days

5. We've been here for _____.
   a. one hour
   b. one o'clock

6. There have been two robberies in our neighborhood since _____.
   a. one month
   b. last month

7. My grandparents have owned this house for _____.
   a. a long time
   b. many years ago

8. They've been in love since _____.
   a. last spring
   b. three months

CHOOSE

1. My right arm has been very _____.
   a. dizzy
   b. stiff

2. My son has a high _____.
   a. fever
   b. pain

3. Tell me, how long has your knee been _____?
   a. nauseous
   b. swollen

4. Ted's leg has been black and _____.
   a. blue
   b. red

5. Dr. Fernando, there are several patients in the _____.
   a. past 24 hours
   b. waiting room

6. Look! I have spots all over my _____!
   a. measles
   b. body

Since I Was a Little Girl

A. Do you know how to ski?

B. Yes. I've known how to ski **since I was a little girl**.

A. Are you two engaged?

B. Yes. We've been engaged **since we finished college**.

1. Does your sister Jennifer play the cello?
since she was eight years old

2. Is your friend Michael a professional musician?
since he graduated from music school

3. Do you have a personal computer?
since I started high school

4. Are you interested in modern art?
since I read about Picasso

5. Is Paul interested in Russian history?
since he visited Moscow

6. Does Timmy know how to count to ten?
since he was two years old

7. Do you like jazz?
since I was a teenager

8. Do you own your own business?
since I got out of the army

9. Do you know Mr. Wilson?
since I was a little boy

10. Do you have termites?
since we bought the house

11. Are you afraid of boats?
since I saw "Titanic"

12. Do your children know about "the birds and the bees"?*
since they were nine years old

*the facts of life

Have You Always Taught History?

A. Have you always taught history?

B. No. **I've taught** history for the past three years. Before that, **I taught** geography.

A. Has Victor always been a taxi driver?

B. No. **He's been** a taxi driver since he immigrated to this country. Before that, **he was** an engineer.

1. Have you always liked classical music?
   the past five years

2. Has Carlos always been the store manager?
   last January

3. Has Kimberly always had short hair?
   she started her new job

4. Has your son always wanted to be an astronaut?
   the past five or six years

5. Has Ron always spoken with a southern accent?
he moved to Georgia

6. Have you and your wife always had a dog?
the last six months

7. Have you always drunk skim milk?
I went on a diet

8. Has Carol always owned a sports car?
she won the lottery

How to Say It!

Reacting to Information

Practice the conversations in this lesson again. React to information in different ways.

How About You?

What is your present address? How long have you lived there?
What was your last address? How long did you live there?

Who is the leader of your country? How long has he/she been the leader?
Who was the last leader of your country? How long was he/she the leader?

Who is your English teacher now? How long has he/she been your teacher?
Who was your last English teacher? How long was he/she your teacher?

READING

A WONDERFUL FAMILY

Mr. and Mrs. Patterson are very proud of their family. Their daughter, Ruth, is a very successful engineer. She has been an engineer since she finished college. Her husband's name is Pablo. They have been happily married for thirty-five years. Pablo is a professional guitarist. He has known how to play the guitar since he was four years old.

Ruth and Pablo have two children. Their son, David, is a computer programmer. He has been interested in computers since he was a teenager. Their daughter, Rita, is a physician. She has been a physician since she finished medical school in 1997.

Mr. and Mrs. Patterson also have a son, Herbert. Herbert is single. He has been a bachelor all his life. He's a famous journalist. They haven't seen him since he moved to Singapore several years ago.

Mr. and Mrs. Patterson feel fortunate to have such wonderful children and grandchildren. They're very proud of them.

✓ READING *CHECK-UP*

TRUE OR FALSE?

1. Ruth got married thirty-five years ago.
2. Ruth's husband is a professional violinist.
3. Ruth and Pablo have two teenagers.
4. The Pattersons' grandson is interested in computers.
5. Rita has been in medical school since 1997.
6. Herbert has never been married.
7. Herbert hasn't seen his parents since they moved to Singapore several years ago.

LISTENING

Listen to the conversation and choose the answer that is true.

1. a. She doesn't have a backache now.
   b. She still has a backache.
2. a. His father is an engineer.
   b. His father isn't an engineer.
3. a. Her knee isn't swollen now.
   b. Her knee is still swollen.
4. a. He isn't a teenager.
   b. He's a teenager.
5. a. She has lived in Tokyo for five years.
   b. She lived in Tokyo for five years.
6. a. Roger lives in Cairo.
   b. Roger has lived in Cairo.
7. a. Amy went home two days ago.
   b. Amy hasn't been home for two days.
8. a. He has lived in Toronto for three years.
   b. He lived in Toronto for three years.

READING

WORKING THEIR WAY UP TO THE TOP

Louis is very successful. For the past six years, he has been the manager of the Big Value Supermarket on Grant Street. Louis has worked very hard to get where he is today. First, he was a clerk for two years. Then, he was a cashier for three years. After that, he was an assistant manager for five years. Finally, six years ago, he became the manager of the store. Everybody at the Big Value Supermarket is very proud of Louis. He started at the bottom, and he has worked his way up to the top.

Kate is very successful. For the past two years, she has been the president of the Marcy Company. Kate has worked very hard to get where she is today. She started her career at the Marcy Department Store in Dallas, Texas. First, she was a salesperson for three years. Then, she was the manager of the Women's Clothing Department for ten years. Then, she was the store manager for eight years. After that, she moved to New York and became a vice president. Finally, two years ago, she became the president. Everybody at the Marcy Company is very proud of Kate. She started at the bottom, and she has worked her way up to the top.

✓ READING *CHECK-UP*

TRUE, FALSE, OR MAYBE?

Answer True, False, or Maybe (if the answer isn't in the story).

1. Louis started as a cashier at the Big Value Supermarket.
2. He has worked there for sixteen years.
3. All employees at the Big Value Supermarket start at the bottom.
4. Kate has been the manager of the Women's Clothing Department in Dallas for ten years.
5. The Women's Clothing Department was on the bottom floor of the store.
6. Kate hasn't been a vice president for two years.

Writing

Write a story about your English teacher.

How long have you known him/her?
How long has he/she been an English teacher?
What did he/she do before that? How long?

Where does he/she live?
How long has he/she lived there?
Has he/she lived anywhere else? Where? How long?

Besides teaching English, what is your English teacher interested in?
How long has he/she been interested in that?

ROLE PLAY *It's Been a Long Time*

A. George!

B. Tony! I can't believe it's you! I haven't seen you in years.

A. That's right, George. It's been a long time. How have you been?

B. Fine. And how about YOU?

A. Everything's fine with me, too.

B. Tell me, Tony, do you still live on Main Street?

A. No. I haven't lived on Main Street for several years. I live on River Road now. And how about YOU? Do you still live on Central Avenue?

B. No. I haven't lived on Central Avenue since 1995. I live on Park Boulevard now.

A. Tell me, George, are you still a barber?

B. No. I haven't been a barber for several years. I'm a computer programmer now. And how about YOU? Are you still a painter?

A. No. I haven't been a painter for a long time. I'm a carpenter now.

B. Tell me, Tony, do you still play the saxophone?

A. No. I haven't played the saxophone for many years. And how about YOU? Do you still go fishing on Saturday mornings?

B. No. I haven't gone fishing on Saturday mornings since I got married.

A. Well, George, I'm afraid I have to go now. We should get together soon.

B. Good idea, Tony. It's been a long time.

Pretend that it's ten years from now. You're walking along the street and suddenly you meet a student who was in your English class. Try this conversation. Remember, you haven't seen this person for ten years.

A. ____________!

B. ____________! I can't believe it's you! I haven't seen you in years.

A. That's right, ____________. It's been a long time. How have you been?

B. Fine. And how about YOU?

A. Everything's fine with me, too.

B. Tell me, ____________, do you still live on ____________?

A. No. I haven't lived on ____________ (for/since) ____________. I live on ____________ now. And how about YOU? Do you still live on ____________?

B. No. I haven't lived on ____________ (for/since) ____________. I live on ____________ now.

A. Tell me, ____________, are you still (a/an) ____________?

B. No. I haven't been (a/an) ____________ (for/since) ____________. I'm (a/an) ____________ now. And how about YOU? Are you still (a/an) ____________?

A. No. I haven't been (a/an) ____________ (for/since) ____________. I'm (a/an) ____________ now.

B. Tell me, ____________, do you still ____________?

A. No. I haven't ____________ (for/since) ____________. And how about YOU? Do you still ____________?

B. No. I haven't ____________ (for/since) ____________.

A. Well, ____________, I'm afraid I have to go now. We should get together soon.

B. Good idea, ____________. It's been a long time.

PRONUNCIATION Reduced *have* & *has*

Listen. Then say it.

How long have you been sick?

How long has Ms. Bennett been a teacher?

Bob has been the manager for six months.

Say it. Then listen.

How long have you known each other?

How long has Mr. Perkins had a stomachache?

Kate has been the president for the past two years.

Write in your journal about your activities and interests. What sport or musical instrument do you play? How long have you known how to play it? Why do you like it? What other things are you interested in? How long have you been interested in those things? Why do you like them?

GRAMMAR FOCUS

Since/For

We've known each other	since	three o'clock. yesterday afternoon. last week. 2000. we were in high school.
	for	three hours. two days. a week. a long time.

Present Perfect vs. Present Tense

I **know** how to ski.

I**'ve known** how to ski since I was a little girl.

Present Perfect vs. Past Tense

Victor **was** an engineer.

He**'s been** a taxi driver since he immigrated.

Choose the correct word.

1. My wife and I (knew have known) each other (since for) 1989.
2. My daughter (is sick has been sick) (since for) several days.
3. How long (have you had do you have) a stomachache?
4. (Are you Have you been) interested in photography now?
5. (We've owned We own) our own business (since for) several years.
6. (She's had She had) a cat (since for) last year. Before that, (she's had she had) a dog.
7. Alexander (was has been) a taxi driver (since for) he came to this country. Before that, (he was he's been) an engineer.
8. I (didn't see haven't seen) you in a long time. How (are have) you been?
9. I (haven't lived didn't live) on Oak Street for many years. (I've lived I live) on Pine Street now.

SIDE by SIDE Gazette

Volume 3 | Number 2

"24/7"
24 Hours a Day/7 Days a Week

Work schedules are changing all over the world

More and more companies around the world are operating twenty-four hours a day, seven days a week. Many of these companies do business with companies in other time zones around the world. Other companies sell products to customers worldwide. In an age of instant communication by telephone, by fax, and over the Internet, many businesses must stay open all the time to serve their customers. International banks, computer companies, manufacturing companies, and businesses that sell their products over the World Wide Web are examples of such companies.

A sign of the times

Employees of these "24/7" companies have seen changes in their work schedules in recent years. About twenty percent of employees don't work on a traditional "9 to 5" daytime schedule anymore. Their companies have switched them to other shifts, such as 3:00 P.M. to 11:00 P.M., or 11:00 P.M. to 7:00 A.M. In the past, many factory workers, doctors and nurses, police, firefighters, and others had these shifts, but now many office workers have also started to work during these hours.

Many local businesses have adjusted their hours to serve the employees of these companies. More and more supermarkets are open 24 hours a day. Restaurants and coffee shops close later and open earlier. And businesses such as photocopy centers, health clubs, laundromats, and even some child-care centers are always open.

Describe the work schedules of people you know. Are there any "24/7" businesses in your area? What's your opinion about these businesses and their employees' work schedules?

The night shift

A typical night at the office

A health club that's open 24 hours a day

A coffee shop that never closes

Late-night shopper at the supermarket

AROUND THE WORLD

Unique Jobs

Some jobs are unique. They exist only in certain countries.

a subway pusher in Japan

a tulip farmer in Holland

a reindeer herder in Siberia

a safari guide in Africa

a coffee plantation worker in Colombia

a dog day-care worker in California

What unique jobs do you know? In what countries do these jobs exist?

Interview

Mr. and Mrs. Roberto Souza have two children, ages two and four. Mr. Souza works the day shift at a manufacturing company, and Mrs. Souza works at night in an office. Their lives are certainly busy!

Q: Mr. Souza, can you describe your typical day?

A: I get up at 5:30 A.M. I take a shower, eat breakfast, and make my lunch. Sometimes I do some laundry before I go to work. I leave the house at 6:30 A.M.

Q: Is anyone in your house awake when you leave?

A: No. Everyone is still asleep. I work from 7:00 A.M. until 3:00 P.M. After work, I pick up my kids at their grandmother's apartment. Usually we go food shopping and then we go home to make dinner. My wife has already left for work. I play with the kids, we eat dinner, and then I put the kids to bed. I'm normally asleep by 10:00 P.M.

Q: And Mrs. Souza, what about your day?

A: The kids and I get up at 7:00. We eat breakfast, and then they play while I do some housework. Sometimes we go to the park or we visit family or friends. Other times we go shopping. I take the kids to my mother's apartment at 2:00 P.M., and I'm at work by 3:00 P.M. I come home at 11:30 P.M. That's my day!

Q: It sounds exhausting! When do you have time to see your husband?

A: Sometimes he waits for me to come home, but usually he has already gone to bed. Believe it or not, we really see each other only on the weekends.

Q: Mr. Souza, what's the most difficult thing about your work schedule?

A: Communication. We leave each other notes and messages about bills, shopping, doctor's appointments, and everything else.

Q: And tell me, Mrs. Souza, is there anything good about these work schedules?

A: Yes. The children are always with a parent or a grandparent. They don't have to go to daycare, which is expensive. We know these schedules won't last forever. When the children are both in school, maybe we can each have a daytime job. I hope so!

FACT FILE

Vacation Time in Different Countries

Employees in different countries have different amounts of vacation time. What's the typical amount of vacation time employees receive in different countries you know? How do people usually spend their vacation time?

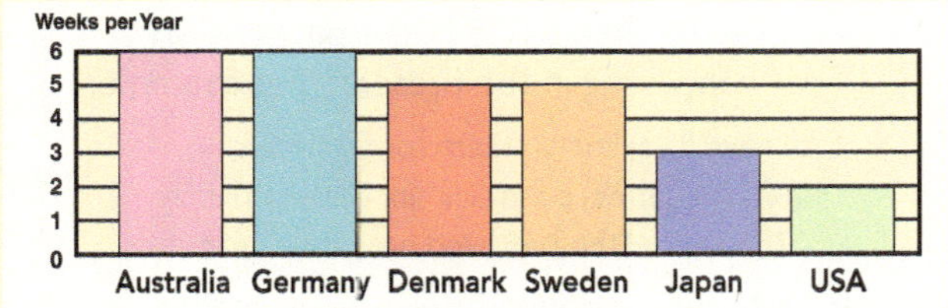

LISTENING

Office Voice Mail

Has Sam . . .

		Yes	No
1	written a note to Mrs. Wilson?	___	___
2	called Mr. Chen?	___	___
3	sent an e-mail about the meeting?	___	___
4	spoken to the custodian?	___	___
5	made a list of the employees?	___	___
6	given the list to Ms. Baxter?	___	___
7	taken the package to the post office?	___	___

FUN with IDIOMS

Do You Know These Expressions?

_d_ 1. My new co-worker is a real peach.

____ 2. She's the top banana in our company.

____ 3. He's a real ham at office parties.

____ 4. He's a couch potato.

____ 5. She's a smart cookie.

____ 6. He wants to ask for a raise, but he's chicken.

a. He's funny.

b. He's afraid.

c. She's intelligent.

d. He's nice.

e. He's lazy.

f. She's the boss.

We've Got Mail!

Dear Side by Side,

We are students in Mr. Smith's class at the English Language Center, and we are very confused! We just don't understand the present perfect tense. We don't have this tense in our languages. We don't know when to use it, and we really don't like all these past participles, such as "given" and "driven." Why do we need this tense anyway? Why can't we just use the tenses we already know?

Sincerely,
"Perfectly Happy with the Present and the Past"

Dear "Perfectly Happy,"

The present perfect tense has always been difficult for learners of English. We'll try to explain it to you with some examples.

We use the present perfect tense to talk about:

- things that happened (or didn't happen) sometime in the past, but the exact time isn't important. For example:

  I have (I've) already seen that movie.*
  He has (He's) never ridden a motorcycle.
  She hasn't gone to the bank yet.

- things that happened many times in the past. For example:

  I have (I've) driven trucks for many years.
  We have (We've) eaten lunch there many times.

- things that happened in the past and are still happening in the present. For example:

  I have (I've) known them for two years.
  She has (She's) been sick since last Thursday.
  They have (They've) lived here for a year.

It's interesting how different languages express time in different ways, and we can understand why this tense is difficult for you. In your languages, you might say:

✗ I live here since last year.
✗ I am living here since last year.
✗ I lived here since last year.

In English, these are all wrong. Sorry! The correct way to say this is:

✓ I have (I've) lived here since last year.

This means "I lived here before, and I still live here now."

So that's why we need the present perfect tense in English. Thanks for your question, and good luck!

Sincerely,
Side by Side

* If the exact time IS important, we use the past tense: "I saw a movie yesterday."

Global Exchange

Alex32: I'm sorry I haven't written for a while. I've been very busy. I've taken four exams this week, and I have to take one more tomorrow. This weekend I'm going to relax. I'm going to see the new Julia Richards movie. (My sister saw it last week, and she says it's one of the best movies she's ever seen.) I'm also going to eat dinner with my family at a new Indian restaurant. I'm looking forward to it. We haven't been to a restaurant in a long time, and I've never eaten Indian food. And I'm going to visit our city's modern art museum. Believe it or not, I've lived here all my life, and I've never gone there! So, how have you been? Have you seen any movies recently? Have you eaten at any restaurants? Have you gone to any interesting places?

Tell a keypal about some things you've done recently.

What Are They Saying?

6

Present Perfect Continuous Tense

- Discussing Duration of Activity
- Reporting Household Repair Problems
- Describing Tasks Accomplished
- Reassuring Someone
- Describing Experiences
- Job Interviews

Vocabulary Preview

1. ask for a raise
2. complain
3. date
4. direct traffic
5. do sit-ups
6. leak
7. look for
8. mend
9. peel
10. pick apples
11. ring
12. stand in line

How Long Have You Been Waiting?

(I have)	I've	been working.
(We have)	We've	
(You have)	You've	
(They have)	They've	
(He has)	He's	
(She has)	She's	
(It has)	It's	

A. How long have you been waiting?

B. I've been waiting **for two hours**.

A. How long has your neighbor's dog been barking?

B. It's been barking **since this morning**.

1. How long has Yasmin been studying English?
eight months

2. How long have Mr. and Mrs. Green been living on School Street?
1994

3. How long has the phone been ringing?
two minutes

4. How long have you been feeling bad?
yesterday morning

5. How long have we been driving?
five hours

6. How long has it been snowing?
late last night

7. How long has Ted been having problems with his back?
high school

8. How long have you been practicing the piano?
half an hour

9. How long have Barry and Susan been dating?
three and a half years

10. How long has your baby son been crying?
early this morning

11. How long have I been running?
twenty minutes

12. How long have we been jogging?
about an hour

They've Been Arguing All Day

Have	I / we / you / they	been working?
Has	he / she / it	

A. What are your neighbors doing?

B. They're arguing.

A. Have they been arguing for a long time?

B. Yes, they have. They've been arguing all day.*

*Or: all morning/all afternoon/all evening/all night

1. *you*
   studying

2. *Gary*
   exercising

3. *Brenda*
   waiting for the bus

4. *your parents*
   watching the news

5. *your car*
   making strange noises

6. *Officer Lopez*
   directing traffic

7. *Jim*
   looking for his keys

8. *you and your friends*
   standing in line for
   concert tickets

9.

READING

APARTMENT PROBLEMS

Mr. and Mrs. Banks have been having a lot of problems in their apartment recently. For several weeks their bedroom ceiling has been leaking, their refrigerator hasn't been working, and the paint in their hallway has been peeling. In addition, they have been taking cold showers since last week because their water heater hasn't been working, and they haven't been sleeping at night because the heating system has been making strange noises.

Mr. and Mrs. Banks are furious. They have been calling the manager of their apartment building every day and complaining about their problems. He has been promising to help them, but they have been waiting for more than a week, and he still hasn't fixed anything at all.

✓ READING *CHECK-UP*

Q & A

Mr. and Mrs. Banks are calling the manager of their apartment building for the first time about each of the problems in their apartment. Using this model, create dialogs based on the story.

A. Hello.
B. Hello. This is *Mrs.* Banks.
A. Yes, *Mrs.* Banks. What can I do for you?
B. We're having a problem with *our bedroom ceiling*.
A. Oh? What's the problem?
B. *It's leaking.*
A. I see. Tell me, how long *has it been leaking?*
B. *It's been leaking for about an hour.*
A. All right, *Mrs.* Banks. I'll take care of it as soon as I can.
B. Thank you.

How About You?

Have you been having problems in your apartment or house recently? Tell about some problems you've been having.

No Wonder They're Tired!

A. You look tired. What have you been doing?

B. I've been writing letters since nine o'clock this morning.

A. Really? How many letters have you written?

B. Believe it or not, I've already written fifteen letters.

A. You're kidding! Fifteen letters?! NO WONDER you're tired!

A. Anthony looks tired. What has he been doing?

B. He's been making pizzas since ten o'clock this morning.

A. Really? How many pizzas has he made?

B. Believe it or not, he's already made seventy-five pizzas.

A. You're kidding! Seventy-five pizzas?! NO WONDER he's tired!

1. *you*
   plant flowers

2. *Ms. Perkins*
   give piano lessons

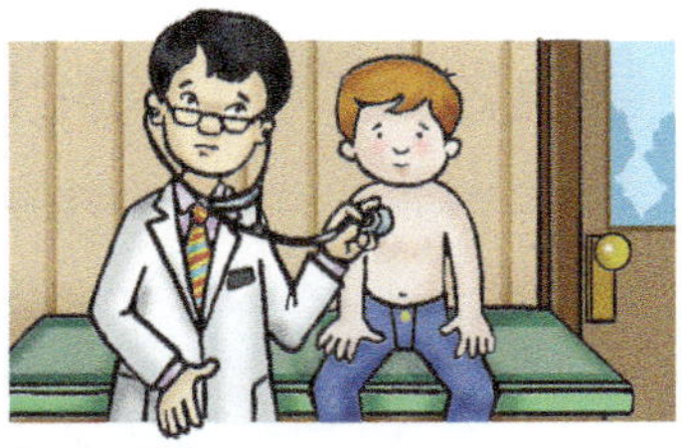

3. *Dr. Chen*
   see patients

4. *your grandmother*
   mend socks

5. *you*
   pick apples

6. *Tom and Sally*
   write thank-you notes

7. *Chester*
   take photographs

8. *Thelma*
   draw pictures

9. *you*
   go to job interviews

10. *Jackie*
    clean cages

11. *Rick*
    do sit-ups

12. *Dr. Harris*
    deliver babies

How to Say It!

Expressing Surprise

Practice the conversations in this lesson again. Express surprise in different ways.

There's Nothing to Be Nervous About!

A. I'm nervous.

B. Why?

A. I'm going to **fly in an airplane** tomorrow, and I've never **flown in an airplane** before.

B. Don't worry! I've been **flying in airplanes** for years. And believe me, there's nothing to be nervous about!

1. *drive downtown*

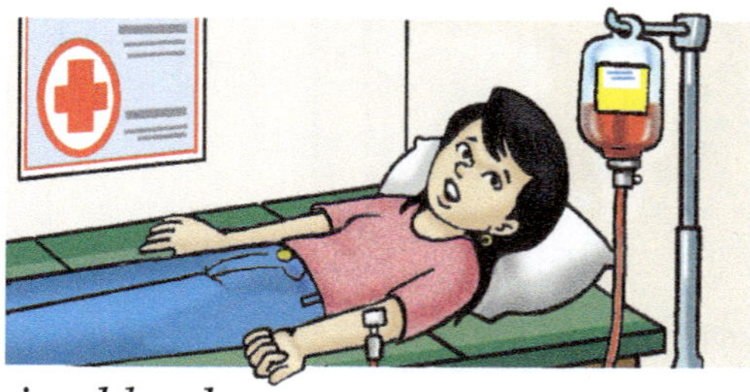

2. *give blood*

3. *buy a used car*

4. *do a chemistry experiment*

5. *run* in a marathon*

6. *go to a job interview*

*run – ran – run

7. *speak at a meeting*

8. *sing in front of an audience*

9. *take a karate lesson*

10. *ask for a raise*

11. *go out on a date*

12.

INTERVIEW *Have You Ever . . . ?*

Interview other students in your class about experiences they have had. Ask these questions and make up your own questions. Then tell the class about these experiences.

Have you ever met a famous person?
(Who did you meet?)

Have you ever spoken at a meeting?
(Where did you speak? What did you say?)

Have you ever been in the hospital?
(Why were you there?)

Have you ever lost something important or valuable?
(What did you lose?)

Have you ever been very embarrassed?
(What happened?)

Have you ever been in an accident?
(What happened?)

ROLE PLAY *At a Job Interview*

Complete this conversation and act it out with another student.

A. Tell me, (Mr./Ms./Mrs./Miss ________), how long have you been living in ________?

B. I've been living in ________ (for/since) ________.

A. And where else have you lived?

B. I've also lived in ________.

A. Oh. How long did you live there?

B. I lived there for ________.

A. Okay. I see here on your resume that you're studying ________.

B. That's correct.

A. How long have you been studying ________?

B. (For/Since) ________.

A. Where?

B. At ________.

A. Tell me about your work experience. Where do you work now?

B. I work at ________.

A. How long have you been working there?

B. I've been working there (for/since) ________.

A. And what do you do there?

B. I ________.

A. And where did you work before that?

B. I worked at ________.

A. How long did you work there?

B. For ________.

A. What did you do?

B. I ________.

A. Well, I don't have any more questions.

B. I appreciate the opportunity to meet with you. Thank you very much.

A. It's been a pleasure. We'll call you soon.

READING

IT'S BEEN A LONG DAY

Frank has been assembling cameras since 7 A.M., and he's very tired. He has assembled 19 cameras today, and he has NEVER assembled that many cameras in one day before! He has to assemble only one more camera, and then he can go home. He's really glad. It's been a long day.

Julie has been typing letters since 9 A.M., and she's very tired. She has typed 25 letters today, and she has NEVER typed that many letters in one day before! She has to type only one more letter, and then she can go home. She's really glad. It's been a very long day.

Officer Jackson has been writing parking tickets since 8 A.M., and he's exhausted! He has written 211 parking tickets today, and he has NEVER written that many parking tickets in one day before! He has to write only one more parking ticket, and then he can go home. He's really glad. It's been an extremely long day.

✓ READING *CHECK-UP*

Q & A

Co-workers are talking with Frank, Julie, and Officer Jackson. Using this model, create dialogs based on the story.

A. *Frank*, you look tired.
B. I am. I've been *assembling cameras* since *7* A.M.
A. Really? How many *cameras* have you *assembled*?
B. Believe it or not, I've already *assembled 19 cameras* today.
A. That's a lot of *cameras*!
B. I know. I've never *assembled* that many *cameras* in one day before!

LISTENING

WHICH WORD DO YOU HEAR?

Listen and choose the correct answer.

1. a. gone b. going
2. a. written b. writing
3. a. seen b. seeing
4. a. taken b. taking
5. a. given b. giving
6. a. driven b. driving

WHO IS SPEAKING?

Listen and decide who is speaking.

1. a. a landlord b. a boss
2. a. a student b. a teacher
3. a. a singer b. a dentist
4. a. a window washer b. a baby-sitter
5. a. a doctor b. a bookkeeper
6. a. a movie theater cashier b. a police officer

PRONUNCIATION Reduced *for*

Listen. Then say it.

I've been working for two hours.

She's been waiting for the bus.

Have you been studying for a long time?

Say it. Then listen.

He's been jogging for thirty minutes.

We've been looking for our keys.

Has she been exercising for a long time?

Write in your journal about places where you have lived, worked, and gone to school.

Where do you live now? How long have you been living there? Where else have you lived? How long did you live there?

Where do you work or go to school now? How long have you been working or going to school there? Where else have you worked or gone to school? How long did you work or study there? What did you do? What did you study?

GRAMMAR FOCUS

Present Perfect Continuous Tense

(I have) (We have) (You have) (They have)	I've We've You've They've	been working.
(He has) (She has) (It has)	He's She's It's	

Have	I we you they	been working?
Has	he she it	

Yes,	I we you they	have.
	he she it	has.

Complete the sentences with *since* or *for* and the correct forms of these verbs.

live	practice	stand	take	write

1. A. How long ______ you and your husband ______ __________ in Los Angeles?
   B. ______ ______ __________ in Los Angeles (since for) three years.
2. A. How long ______ your daughter ______ __________ the piano?
   B. ______ ______ __________ the piano (since for) 9:00 A.M.
3. A. ______ your friends ______ __________ in line for a long time?
   B. Yes, ______ ______. ______ ______ __________ in line (since for) about an hour.
4. Ms. Lee ______ ______ __________ photographs (since for) early this morning.
   ______ already __________ more than fifty photographs!
5. I'm very busy. ______ ______ __________ letters (for since) five hours.
   ______ already __________ twenty letters!

7

Gerunds
Infinitives
Review: Present Perfect and Present Perfect Continuous Tenses

- Discussing Recreation Preferences
- Discussing Things You Dislike Doing
- Habits
- Describing Talents and Skills
- Telling About Important Decisions

Vocabulary Preview

1 
2 
3 
4 
5 
6 
7 
8 
9 
10 

1. enjoy/like
2. hate/can't stand
3. avoid
4. begin/start
5. continue/keep on
6. quit/stop
7. consider/think about
8. decide
9. learn
10. practice

My Favorite Way to Relax

to watch	watching
to dance	dancing
to swim	swimming

A. Do you **like to watch TV**?

B. Yes. I **enjoy watching TV** very much. **Watching TV** is my favorite way to relax.

1. *you*
   paint

2. *Beverly*
   knit

3. *Kevin*
   swim

4. *your parents*
   play golf

5. *you and your friends*
   dance

6. *you*
   listen to music

7. *Hector*
   go to the movies

8. *Valerie*
   browse the web

9.

READING

ENJOYING LIFE

Howard enjoys reading. He likes to read in the park. He likes to read in the library. He even likes to read in the bathtub! As you can see, reading is a very important part of Howard's life.

Patty enjoys singing. She likes to sing in school. She likes to sing in church. She even likes to sing in the shower! As you can see, singing is a very important part of Patty's life.

Brenda enjoys watching TV. She likes to watch TV in the living room. She likes to watch TV in bed. She even likes to watch TV in department stores! As you can see, watching TV is a very important part of Brenda's life.

Tom enjoys talking about politics. He likes to talk about politics with his friends. He likes to talk about politics with his parents. He even likes to talk about politics with his barber! As you can see, talking about politics is a very important part of Tom's life.

✓ READING *CHECK-UP*

Q & A

The people in the story are introducing themselves to you at a party. Using this model, create dialogs based on the story.

A. Hello. My name is *Howard*.
B. Nice to meet you. My name is ______.
Are you enjoying the party?
A. Not really. To tell you the truth, I'd rather be *reading*.
B. Oh? Do you like to *read*?
A. Oh, yes. I enjoy *reading* very much.
B. I like to *read*, too. In fact, *reading* is my favorite way to relax.
A. Mine, too. Tell me, what do you like to *read*?
B. I like to *read books about famous people*. How about you?
A. I enjoy *reading short stories*.
B. Well, please excuse me. I have to go now. It was nice meeting you.
A. Nice meeting you, too.

She Hates to Drive Downtown

{like to work / like working} {hate to work / hate working} {—— / avoid working}

A. Does Helen **like** {**to drive** / **driving**} downtown?

B. No. She **hates** {**to drive** / **driving**}* downtown.

She **avoids driving** downtown whenever she can.

* Or: can't stand {to drive / driving}

1. *Albert*
   travel by plane

2. *you*
   go to the mall

3. *your parents*
   eat at fast-food restaurants

4. *Carmen*
   sit in the sun

5. *you and your friends*
   talk about politics

6. *Kathy*
   use her cell phone

7. *you*
   wear a suit and tie

8. *the president*
   talk to reporters

9.

How About You?

What do you enjoy doing?
What do you avoid doing whenever you can?

READING

BAD HABITS

Jill's co-workers always tell her to stop eating junk food. They think that eating junk food is unhealthy. Jill knows that, but she still keeps on eating junk food. She wants to stop, but she can't. Eating junk food is a habit she just can't break.

Vincent's friends always tell him to stop gossiping. They think that gossiping isn't nice. Vincent knows that, but he still keeps on gossiping. He wants to stop, but he can't. Gossiping is a habit he just can't break.

Jennifer's parents always tell her to stop interrupting people while they're talking. They think that interrupting people is very rude. Jennifer knows that, but she still keeps on interrupting people. She wants to stop, but she can't. Interrupting people is a habit she just can't break.

Walter's wife always tells him to stop talking about business all the time. She thinks that talking about business all the time is boring. Walter knows that, but he still keeps on talking about business. He wants to stop, but he can't. Talking about business is a habit he just can't break.

✓ READING *CHECK-UP*

Q & A

You're talking with the people in the story about their bad habits. Using this model, create dialogs based on the story.

A. *Jill?*
B. Yes?
A. You know . . . I don't mean to be critical, but I really think you should stop *eating junk food.*
B. Oh?
A. Yes. *Eating junk food is unhealthy.* Don't you think so?
B. You're right. The truth is . . . I want to stop, but I can't. *Eating junk food* is a habit I just can't break.

How About You?

Do you have any habits you "just can't break"? Tell about them.

How Did You Learn to Swim So Well?

start to swim **start** swimm**ing**	**learn to** swim ——	—— **practice** swimm**ing**

A. How did you **learn to swim** so well?

B. Well, I **started** { **to swim** / **swimming** } when I was young, and I've been **swimming** ever since.

A. I envy you. I've never **swum** before.

B. I'll be glad to teach you how.

A. Thank you. But isn't **swimming** very difficult?

B. Not at all. After you **practice swimming** a few times, you'll probably **swim** as well as I do.

A. How did you learn to __________ so well?

B. Well, I started { to __________ / __________ing } when I was young,

and I've been __________ing ever since.

A. I envy you. I've never __________ before.

B. I'll be glad to teach you how.

A. Thank you. But isn't __________ing very difficult?

B. Not at all. After you practice __________ing a few times,

you'll probably __________ as well as I do.

1. *draw*

2. *box*

3. *surf*

4. *figure skate*

5. *tap dance*

6.

How to Say It!

Expressing Appreciation

Practice the conversations in this lesson again. Express appreciation in different ways.

Guess What I've Decided to Do!

{ **decide to** buy / ——— } { ——— / **consider** buying } { ——— / **think about** buying }

A. Guess what I've decided to do!

B. What?

A. I've **decided to get married**.

B. That's wonderful! How long have you been **thinking about getting married**?

A. For a long time, actually. I **considered getting married** a few years ago, but never did.

B. Well, I think you're making the right decision. **Getting married** is a great idea.

A. Guess what I've decided to do!

B. What?

A. I've decided to ________.

B. That's wonderful! How long have you been thinking about ________ing?

A. For a long time, actually. I considered ________ing a few years ago, but never did.

B. Well, I think you're making the right decision. ________ing is a great idea.

1. *get a dog*

2. *buy a new car*

3. *move to New York*

4. *go on a diet*

5. *go back to college*

6. *start my own business*

7. *retire*

8. *become a vegetarian*

9.

I've Made a Decision

begin to eat **begin** eating	—— **keep on** eating	—— **quit** eating
start to eat **start** eating	**continue to** eat **continue** eating	—— **stop** eating
begin = start	keep on = continue	quit = stop

A. I've made a decision.

B. What is it?

A. I've decided to **quit eating** junk food.

B. That's great! Have you ever tried to **stop eating** junk food before?

A. Yes. Many times. But every time I've **stopped eating** it, I've **begun*** {**to eat** / **eating**} it again after a few days.

B. Well, I hope you're successful this time.

A. I hope so, too. After all, I can't **keep on eating** junk food for the rest of my life.

* begin – began – begun

A. I've made a decision.

B. What is it?

A. I've decided to quit* ____________ing.

B. That's great! Have you ever tried to stop* ____________ing before?

A. Yes. Many times. But every time I've stopped* ____________ing,

I've begun* { to ____________ / ____________ing } again after a few days.

B. Well, I hope you're successful this time.

A. I hope so, too. After all, I can't keep on* ____________ing for the rest of my life.

* quit = stop
begin = start
keep on = continue

1. *bite my nails*

2. *tease my little sister*

3. *worry about my health*

4. *argue with my neighbors*

5. *complain about my son-in-law*

6.

READING

IMPORTANT DECISIONS

Jim had to make an important decision recently. He made an appointment for an interview at the Tektron Internet Company, and he had to decide what to wear. First, he considered wearing a sweater to the interview. Then, he thought about wearing a sports jacket. Finally, he decided to wear a suit and tie. Jim thinks he made the right decision. He's glad he didn't wear a sweater or sports jacket. He feels that wearing a suit and tie was the best thing to do.

Emily had to make an important decision recently. Her landlord sold her apartment building, and she had to decide where to move. First, she considered moving to another apartment. Then, she thought about buying a small house. Finally, she decided to move home with her parents for a while. Emily thinks she made the right decision. She's glad she didn't move to another apartment or buy a small house. She thinks that moving home with her parents for a while was the right thing to do.

Nick had to make an important decision recently. He got out of the army, and he had to decide what to do next with his life. First, he considered working in his family's grocery store. Then, he thought about taking a job in a restaurant. Finally, he decided to enroll in college and study engineering. Nick thinks he made the right decision. He's glad he didn't work in his family's grocery store or take a job in a restaurant. He feels that enrolling in college and studying engineering was the smartest thing to do.

Maria had to make an important decision recently. She lost her job as a bookkeeper because her company went out of business, and she had to decide what to do. First, she considered looking for another job as a bookkeeper. Then, she thought about working as a secretary for a while. Finally, she decided to enroll in technical school and study network programming. Maria thinks she made the right decision. She's glad she didn't look for another job as a bookkeeper or work as a secretary for a while. She thinks that enrolling in technical school and studying network programming was the best thing to do.

READING *CHECK-UP*

TRUE, FALSE, OR MAYBE?

Answer True, False, or Maybe (if the answer isn't in the story).

1. Jim considered wearing a sweater to the interview.
2. He got the job at the Tektron Internet Company.
3. Emily decided not to move to another apartment.
4. Emily never considered buying a small house.
5. Emily's parents think that moving home was the right thing for her to do.
6. Nick's family is in the restaurant business.
7. Nick first became interested in engineering while he was in the army.
8. Maria wasn't a very good bookkeeper.
9. After Maria lost her job, she worked as a secretary for a while.
10. Maria feels she made the right decision.

LISTENING

Listen and choose the correct answer.

1. a. She enjoys going to the mall.
   b. She hates going to the mall.
2. a. He sold his car.
   b. He's going to sell his car.
3. a. He bites his nails.
   b. He stopped biting his nails.
4. a. She likes traveling by plane.
   b. She can't stand traveling by plane.
5. a. They're going to move to Florida.
   b. They might move to Florida.
6. a. He's married.
   b. He isn't married.
7. a. She's going to keep on practicing.
   b. She isn't going to continue practicing.
8. a. He interrupts people.
   b. He doesn't interrupt people any more.

PRONUNCIATION Reduced *to*

Listen. Then say it.

I like to watch TV.

She hates to drive downtown.

How did you learn to draw?

I started to skate last year.

Say it. Then listen.

We decided to move.

He can't stand to wear a tie.

They've already begun to eat.

I continue to worry about my health.

Write in your journal about an important decision you had to make.

I had to make an important decision recently.

__________________________________,

and I had to decide what to do. First, I considered

____________. *Then, I thought about* ____________.

Finally, I decided to __________________ *because*

__________________________________.

GRAMMAR FOCUS

Verb + Infinitive

decide learn	to ____

Verb + Gerund

avoid consider enjoy keep on practice quit stop think about	____ing

Verb + Infinitive/Gerund

begin can't stand continue hate like start	to ____ ____ing

Gerund as Subject

Watching TV is my favorite way to relax.

Gerund as Object

I'm thinking about **getting married.**

Choose the correct word.

1. I enjoy (to listen listening) to music.
2. My daughter practices (to skate skating) every weekend.
3. We've decided (to move moving) to Florida.
4. I usually avoid (to talk talking) about politics.
5. I really want to quit (to bite biting) my nails.
6. You can't keep on (to worry worrying) all the time.
7. Where did you learn (to draw drawing) so well?
8. I know I have to stop (to eat eating) junk food.

8

Past Perfect Tense
Past Perfect Continuous Tense

- Discussing Things People Had Done
- Discussing Preparations for Events
- Describing Consequences of Being Late
- Discussing Feelings
- Describing Accomplishments

VOCABULARY PREVIEW

1. discuss
2. fly a kite
3. go canoeing
4. go window-shopping
5. pack
6. purchase
7. realize
8. shine
9. water
10. wrestle
11. forget
12. remember
13. memorize
14. rehearse
15. perform

They Didn't Want to

I He She It We You They	had eaten.

A. Why didn't Mr. and Mrs. Henderson **see** a movie last weekend?

B. They didn't want to. They **had seen** a movie the weekend before.

1. Why didn't your parents eat out yesterday evening?

2. Why didn't Barry go canoeing last Saturday?

3. Why didn't Martha make eggs for breakfast yesterday morning?

4. Why didn't you have pizza for dinner last night?

5. Why didn't you and your friends drive to the beach last Sunday?

6. Why didn't Paul wear his polka dot shirt to work yesterday?

7. Why didn't Susan take a psychology course last semester?

8. Why didn't your neighbors give a party last month?

9. Why didn't Mozart write an opera last week?

10. Why didn't you go window-shopping last Saturday afternoon?

11. Why didn't Monica fly her kite yesterday?

12. Why didn't you and your family discuss politics at the dinner table yesterday evening?

13. Why didn't George do card tricks for his friends last weekend?

14.

READING

THE MOST IMPORTANT THING

Roger thought he was all prepared for his dinner party last night. He had sent invitations to his boss and all the people at the office. He had looked through several cookbooks and had found some very interesting recipes. He had even gone all the way downtown to buy imported fruit, vegetables, and cheese, which he needed for his dinner. However, as soon as Roger's doorbell rang and his guests arrived, he realized that he had forgotten to turn on the oven. Roger felt very foolish. He couldn't believe what he had done. He thought he was all prepared for his dinner party, but he had forgotten to do the most important thing.

Mr. and Mrs. Jenkins thought they were all prepared for their vacation. They had packed their suitcases several days ahead of time. They had gone to the bank and purchased traveler's checks. They had even asked their next-door neighbor to water their plants, feed their dog, and shovel their driveway if it snowed. However, as soon as Mr. and Mrs. Jenkins arrived at the airport, they realized that they had forgotten to bring their plane tickets with them, and there wasn't enough time to go back home and get them. Mr. and Mrs. Jenkins were heartbroken. They couldn't believe what they had done. They thought they were all prepared for their vacation, but they had forgotten to do the most important thing.

Harold thought he was all prepared for his job interview yesterday. He had gone to his barber and gotten a very short haircut. He had bought a new shirt, put on his best tie, and shined his shoes. He had even borrowed his brother's new suit. However, as soon as Harold began the job interview, he realized that he had forgotten to bring along his resume. Harold was furious with himself. He thought he was all prepared for his job interview, but he had forgotten to do the most important thing.

Janet thought she was all prepared for the school play. She had memorized the script several weeks in advance. She had practiced her songs and dances until she knew them perfectly. She had even stayed up all night the night before and rehearsed the play by herself from beginning to end. However, as soon as the curtain went up and the play began, Janet realized that she had forgotten to put on her costume. Janet was really embarrassed. She couldn't believe what she had done. She thought she was all prepared for the play, but she had forgotten to do the most important thing.

✓ READING *CHECK-UP*

True, False, or Maybe?

Answer True, False, or Maybe (if the answer isn't in the story).

1. Roger had remembered to buy the ingredients he needed.
2. Roger hadn't remembered to cook the food.
3. Roger's guests couldn't believe what he had done.
4. Mr. and Mrs. Jenkins had forgotten to buy their plane tickets.
5. When Mr. and Mrs. Jenkins realized what had happened, they felt very sad and upset.
6. Harold thinks it's important to bring a resume to a job interview.
7. Harold doesn't have a suit.
8. Janet hadn't seen the script until the night before the play.
9. Before the play began, Janet hadn't realized that she had forgotten to put on her costume.

Which Is Correct?

1. Before Barbara went on her vacation, she went to the bank and bought (tickets traveler's checks).
2. Peter wanted his boss to come over for dinner, but he forgot to send him (a resume an invitation).
3. Sheila (borrowed bought) her roommate's laptop for a few days.
4. Our grandchildren were (heartbroken foolish) when our dog ran away.
5. At the supermarket next to the United Nations, (imported important) people buy (imported important) food.

How About You?

Have you ever thought you were all prepared for something, but you realized you had forgotten to do something important?

What were you preparing for?
What had you done?
What had you forgotten to do?

They Didn't Get There on Time

A. Did you get to the **concert** on time?

B. No, I didn't. By the time I got to the **concert**, it had already **begun**.

1. *post office*
close

2. *plane*
take off

3. *movie*
start

4. *train*
leave

5. *lecture*
end

6. *meeting*
finish

7. *library*
close

8. *boat*
sail away

9. *parade*
go by

He Hadn't Gone Fishing in a Long Time

A. Did Grandpa enjoy **going fishing** last weekend?

B. Yes, he did. He hadn't **gone fishing** in a long time.

1. Did Natalie enjoy swimming in the ocean last weekend?

2. Did you enjoy seeing a movie yesterday evening?

3. Did Mr. and Mrs. Ramirez enjoy taking a walk along the beach yesterday?

4. Did you and your friends enjoy eating at Burger Queen yesterday?

5. Did Henry enjoy singing with the choir last Sunday?

6. Did you enjoy having strawberry shortcake for dessert last night?

7. Did Jim and Tess enjoy riding on a roller coaster this afternoon?

8. Did Kevin enjoy playing "hide and seek" with his children last night?

9. Did Mrs. Kramer enjoy reading her old love letters last weekend?

READING

DAYS GONE BY

Michael took a very special trip last month. He went back to Fullerton, his home town. Michael's visit to Fullerton was very special to him. He was born there, he grew up there, but he hadn't been back there since he finished high school.

He went to places he hadn't gone to in years. He walked through the park in the center of town and remembered the days he had walked through the same park with his first girlfriend. He passed by the empty field where he and his friends had played baseball every day after school. And he stood for a while in front of the movie theater and thought about all the Saturday afternoons he had spent there sitting in the balcony, watching his favorite movie heroes and eating popcorn.

He did things he hadn't done in a long time. He had some homemade ice cream at the ice cream shop, he rode on the merry-go-round in the park, and he went fishing at the lake on the outskirts of town. For a while, he felt like a kid again. He hadn't had homemade ice cream, ridden on a merry-go-round, or gone fishing since he was a young boy.

He also saw people he hadn't seen in years. He visited several of his old neighbors who had never moved out of the neighborhood. He said hello to the owners of the candy store near his house. And he even bumped into Mrs. Riley, his tenth-grade science teacher.

During his visit to his home town, Michael remembered places he hadn't gone to, things he hadn't done, and people he hadn't seen since his childhood. Michael's trip back to Fullerton was a very nostalgic experience for him. Going back to Fullerton brought back many memories of days gone by.

READING *CHECK-UP*

TRUE, FALSE, OR MAYBE?

Answer True, False, or Maybe (if the answer isn't in the story).

1. Michael moved back to Fullerton last month.
2. He hadn't seen Fullerton in years.
3. When Michael passed by the field last month, children were playing baseball.
4. Michael enjoyed going to the movies when he was young.
5. The ice cream shop was near Michael's home in Fullerton.
6. Michael rode on the merry-go-round when he was a young boy.
7. Some of Michael's old neighbors still live in the same neighborhood.
8. Mrs. Riley still teaches science.

WHICH IS CORRECT?

1. I always enjoy eating Aunt Betty's (home town   homemade) food.
2. The new shopping mall is located in the (outskirts   outside) of our city.
3. She recently visited the town where she had (spent   grown up) her childhood.
4. I bumped (through   into) an old friend on the street the other day.
5. They hadn't been (back   by) to their old neighborhood in several years.
6. Seeing my old college friends was a (nauseous   nostalgic) experience for me.

LISTENING

Listen and choose the correct answer.

1. a. Yes. They've never eaten there.
   b. Yes. They had never eaten there.
2. a. I had already seen it.
   b. I've already seen it.
3. a. No. It had already started.
   b. No. It has already started.
4. a. But I had already done it.
   b. But I've already done it.
5. a. She had memorized all the important names and dates.
   b. She's going to study very hard.
6. a. Have you ever stayed there before?
   b. Had you ever stayed there before?

THINK ABOUT IT! *Feelings and Experiences*

Think about times you have had these feelings. Share your experiences with other students.

Have You Heard About Harry?

A. Have you heard about Harry?

B. No, I haven't. What happened?

A. He broke his leg last week.

B. That's terrible! How did he do THAT?

A. He was roller-skating . . . and he had never roller-skated before.

B. Poor Harry! I hope he feels better soon.

A. Have you heard about __________?

B. No, I haven't. What happened?

A. (He/She) __________ last week.

B. That's terrible! How did (he/she) do THAT?

A. (He/She) was __________ing . . . and (he/she) had never ________ before.

B. Poor __________! I hope (he/she) feels better soon.

1. *twist his ankle*
   fly a kite

2. *injure her knee*
   ski

3. *burn himself*
   bake brownies

4. *sprain her wrist*
play squash

5. *get a black eye*
box

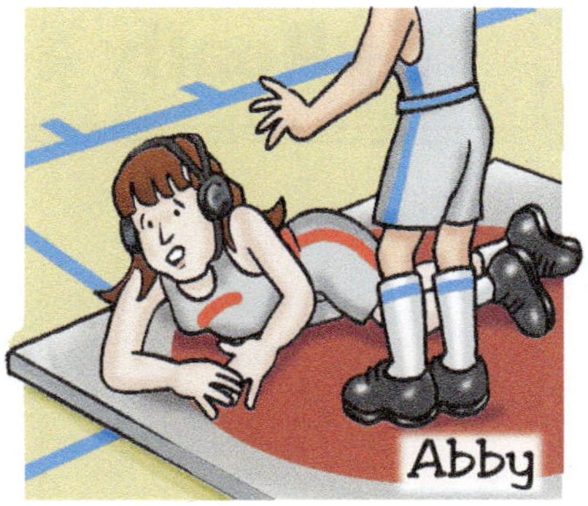

6. *hurt her arm*
wrestle

7. *lose his voice*
sing opera

8. *dislocate her shoulder*
do gymnastics

9. *get hurt in an accident*
ride a motorcycle

10. *sprain his back*
do the tango

11. *break his front teeth*
chew on a steak bone

12.

How to Say It!

Sharing News About Someone

A. { Have you heard about / Have you heard the news about / Have you heard what happened to } *Harry?*

B. No, I haven't. What happened?

Practice the conversations in this lesson again. Begin your conversations in different ways.

It's Really a Shame

I He She It We You They	had been eating.

A. I heard that Arnold failed his driver's test last week. Is it true?

B. Yes, it is . . . and it's really a shame. He had been practicing for a long time.

A. I heard that ____________________ last week. Is it true?

B. Yes, it is . . . and it's really a shame. (He/She/They) had been ____________ing for a long time.

I heard that . . .

1. Fred lost his job at the factory
work there

2. Larry and Jane broke up
go together

3. Mona had to cancel her trip to France
plan it

4. Pam and Bob canceled their wedding
plan to get married

5. Mr. and Mrs. Williams moved
live in this neighborhood

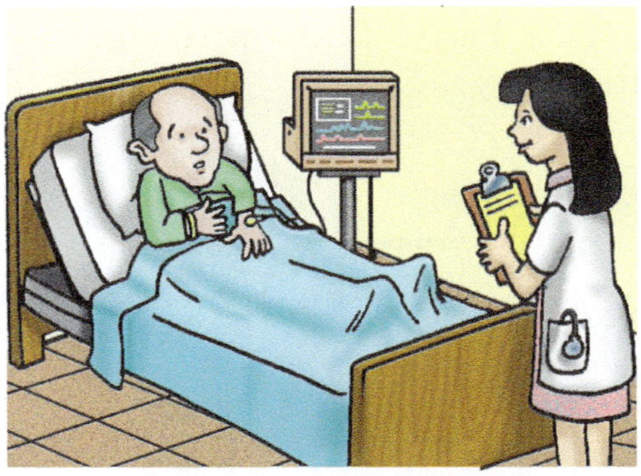

6. Walter had another heart attack
feel better

7. Alex did poorly on his science exam
study for it

8. Penny twisted her ankle and couldn't run in the marathon
train for it

9. Your daughter got sick and couldn't perform in her piano recital
rehearse for it

10. Herbert caught a cold and couldn't go camping
look forward to it

READING

THEIR PLANS "FELL THROUGH"

Patty had planned to have a party last weekend. She had been getting ready for the party for a long time. She had invited all of her friends and several co-workers, she had cooked lots of food, and she had cleaned her apartment from top to bottom. But at the last minute, she got sick and had to cancel the party. Poor Patty! She was really disappointed.

Michael had planned to ask his boss for a raise last week. He had been preparing to ask his boss for a raise for a long time. He had come to work early for several weeks, he had worked late at the office every night, and he had even bought a new suit to wear to the appointment with his boss. Unfortunately, before Michael could even ask for a raise, his boss fired him.

John and Julia had planned to get married last month. They had been planning their wedding for more than a year, and all of their friends and relatives had been looking forward to the ceremony. Julia had bought a beautiful wedding gown, John had rented a fancy tuxedo, and they had sent invitations to 150 people. But at the last minute, John "got cold feet"* and they had to cancel the wedding.

* got scared

IN YOUR OWN WORDS

FOR WRITING AND DISCUSSION

Tell about plans YOU had that "fell through."

What had you planned to do?
How long had you been planning to do it?
What had you done beforehand?
What went wrong? What happened?
Were you upset? disappointed?

ON YOUR OWN *Accomplishments*

When Stella Karp won the marathon last week, nobody was surprised. She had been getting up early and jogging every morning. She had been eating health foods and taking vitamins for several months. And she had been swimming fifty laps every day after work. Stella Karp really deserved to win the marathon. After all, she had been preparing for it for a long time.

When my friend Stuart finally passed his driver's test the other day, nobody was surprised. He had been taking lessons at the driving school for several months. He had been practicing driving with his father for the past several weeks. And he had been studying the "rules of the road" since he was a little boy. My friend Stuart really deserved to pass his driver's test. After all, he had been preparing for it for a long time.

When Sally Compton got a promotion last week, nobody was surprised. She had been working overtime every day for several months. She had been studying computer programming in the evening. And she had even been taking extra work home on the weekends. Sally Compton really deserved to get a promotion. After all, she had been working hard to earn it for a long time.

We all feel proud when we accomplish something that we have prepared for. Tell other students about an accomplishment you're proud of.

Write in your journal about something you accomplished: What did you accomplish? How long had you been preparing for it? How had you been preparing?

PRONUNCIATION Reduced *had*

Listen. Then say it.

She had seen a movie the day before.

We had never roller-skated before.

It had already begun.

Patty had planned to have a party.

Say it. Then listen.

He had gone fishing the week before.

We had been studying for several hours.

I had forgotten to do it.

Tom had been practicing for a long time.

GRAMMAR FOCUS

Past Perfect Tense

I He She It We You They	had eaten.

I He She It We You They	hadn't eaten.

Past Perfect Continuous Tense

I He She It We You They	had been eating.

Complete the conversations. Use the correct forms of these verbs in your answers.

forget	go	have	live	plan	play	ride	see	take off	work

1. A. Why didn't you see a movie last weekend?
   B. I didn't want to. _____ _____ _________ a movie the weekend before.
2. A. Why was your brother upset during his job interview yesterday?
   B. _____ _____ _________ to bring along his resume.
3. A. Did your daughter enjoy having chocolate cake for dessert last night?
   B. Yes, she did. _____ _____ _________ chocolate cake for dessert in a long time.
4. A. Did you get to the airport on time?
   B. No, I didn't. By the time I got to the airport, the plane _____ already _________.
5. A. Why didn't your friends go sailing with us last Sunday?
   B. They didn't want to. _____ _____ _________ sailing the weekend before.
6. A. How did Roberta hurt herself?
   B. She was _____ a motorcycle, and _____ _____ never _________ a motorcycle before.
7. A. Did you hear that Gregory and Isabelle canceled their wedding?
   B. No, I didn't. What a shame! _____ _____ _____ _________ it for a long time.
8. A. Is it true that Bruno lost his job at the factory?
   B. Yes, it is . . . and it's really a shame. _____ _____ _____ _________ there for many years.
9. A. Did you and your friends enjoy playing basketball yesterday?
   B. Yes, we did. _____ _____ _________ basketball in a long time.
10. A. Did you hear that Mrs. Ramirez moved last weekend?
    B. Yes, I did. I'm really surprised. _____ _____ _____ _________ here for more than thirty years.

SIDE by SIDE Gazette

Volume 3 Number 3

The Jamaican Bobsled Team

Amazing athletes from a Caribbean island

An unusual group of athletes arrived in Calgary, Canada for the 1988 Winter Olympic Games—the Jamaican Bobsled Team. Many people were surprised. How could the Caribbean island of Jamaica have a bobsled team? Jamaica doesn't have any snow!

The Jamaican athletes had never competed in the Winter Olympics before. In fact, most of them hadn't ever been on a bobsled or seen snow before they began to prepare for the Olympics. But by the time the team members arrived in Calgary, they had trained hard for their first Olympic event. They had been running and weight training in Jamaica. Then they had gone to a training center in Lake Placid, New York. Unfortunately, they had poor equipment, and their bobsled crashed a lot during training.

They didn't do well in the Olympics. Most people were sure they had seen the Jamaican Bobsled Team for the first and last time! But the team didn't give up. They had lost, but they had been in the Olympics, and they wanted to go back and compete again.

The team went to a special training center in Germany. They trained there four to eight hours a day. By the time these athletes arrived at the 1994 Olympic Winter Games in Lillehammer, France, they had become a much stronger bobsled team. They had practiced for years. They were also very famous because a movie about the team, *Cool Runnings*, had been in theaters around the world the year before.

At the 1994 games, the team came in 14th in the four-person bobsled event, and they placed 10th in the two-person event. The team had done the impossible! They had competed well in the Olympics, and they had won the hearts of fans around the world.

The movie *Cool Runnings* tells the story of a Jamaican bobsled team at the Olympics. The movie is part fact and part fiction. The popular movie soundtrack has reggae music by famous Jamaican musicians.

The first modern Olympics were in Athens, Greece in 1896. Now there are Summer Olympics and Winter Olympics every four years. Athletes represent their countries in different events. Summer Olympic events include track, gymnastics, and swimming. Winter Olympic events include skiing, skating, and the bobsled competition.

AROUND THE WORLD

Children and Sports Training

In different countries around the world, children begin training at an early age to compete in different popular sports.

hockey in Canada

baseball in Japan

soccer in Brazil

gymnastics in Russia

basketball in the United States

distance running in Kenya

What sports are popular in your country? At what age do children start training to compete in these sports?

Interview

A Side by Side Gazette reporter interviewed Olga Petrova last week. Olga had just won the Women's Regional Figure Skating Competition.

Q: **Olga, I'm sure you're very happy about today's competition.**

A: Oh, yes. I'm very happy. You know, I had been preparing for this day for a long time.

Q: **How had you been preparing?**

A: In the months before the competition, I had been training with my coach ten hours a day. I had been getting up early, and I had been practicing my routines over and over again.

Q: **When did you first know you wanted to compete as a skater?**

A: I began to skate back in Russia when I was four years old. By the time I was seven, I had already skated in many competitions, and I had won several medals. We moved here when I was ten, and I began to take lessons at a skating program in our city. By the time I was eleven, I had finished all the levels of this program. My parents found a professional coach, Mr. Gary Abrams, and I've been training with him ever since.

Q: **Now that you have won this regional competition, what's next?**

A: The National Competition. It's in three months. I have to work very hard to prepare for that. My dream is to be in the Olympics next winter. I must do very well in the Nationals.

Q: **Good luck, Olga! We'll see you in the Olympics!**

A: Oh, I hope so.

FACT FILE

Countries in the Olympics

Only 14 countries competed in the first modern Olympics in 1896. Over the years, the number of participating countries has grown. Does your country compete in the summer or winter games? In which events does your country do well?

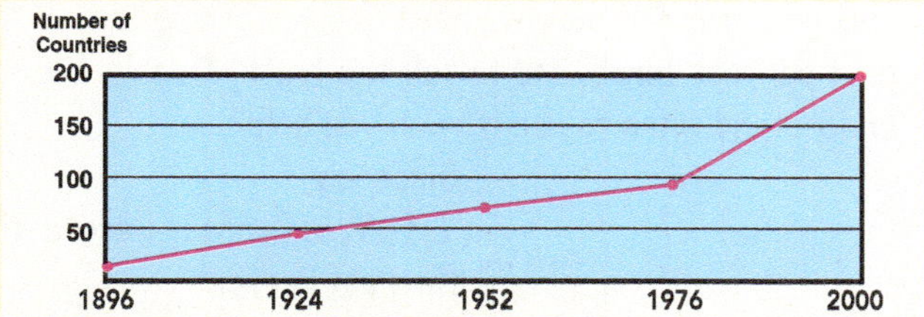

LISTENING

Olympic Game Highlights

b	1	a. figure skating
___	2	b. basketball
___	3	c. running
___	4	d. gymnastics
___	5	e. swimming

FUN with IDIOMS

Do You Know These Expressions?

c	1. Break a leg!	a. Don't be sad!
___	2. Hold your tongue!	b. Try hard!
___	3. Keep your chin up!	c. Good luck!
___	4. Keep your eye on the ball!	d. Pay attention!
___	5. Put your best foot forward!	e. Don't bother me!
___	6. Get off my back!	f. Be quiet!

We've Got Mail!

Dear Side by Side,

I have a question about gerunds and infinitives after verbs. I'm very confused. I know that after some verbs, I must use a gerund, such as "practice swimming" and "consider buying." After other verbs, I must use an infinitive, such as "learn to swim" and "decide to buy." And finally, I know that after some verbs, I can use either a gerund or an infinitive, such as "like to swim" and "like swimming." Are there any rules that will tell me what to do with different verbs?

Sincerely,
"Worrying About the Rules"

Dear "Worrying About the Rules,"

You seem to understand how to use gerunds and infinitives. Unfortunately, we're sorry to tell you that there aren't any rules about what to do with different verbs. You just have to learn about each verb. Keep on practicing gerunds and infinitives, and stop worrying about the rules! Using these verbs is a lot better than thinking about them too much! Good luck!

Sincerely,
Side by Side

Dear Side by Side,

We've been studying the present perfect and present perfect continuous tenses in our class for the past several weeks. I think I finally understand this grammar, but now we have begun learning the past perfect tense, and to tell the truth, I don't understand when to use it. Can you help?

Sincerely,
"Life Was Perfect Before the Past Perfect"

Dear "Life Was Perfect,"

We understand your problem because we use both the present perfect and past perfect tenses to talk about things that happened in the past. Here's the difference. We use the present perfect tense to talk about things that happened before now. For example:

I don't want to see that movie today.
I have already seen it.

We use the past perfect tense to talk about things that happened before another time in the past. For example:

I didn't want to see that movie yesterday.
I had already seen it.

We're glad you have learned the present perfect tense, and we're sure you'll do well with the past perfect!

Best wishes,
Side by Side

Global Exchange

Stamp4: Have I told you about my hobby? I've been collecting stamps since I was a little kid. I began to collect stamps when I was eight years old. At that time, my mother worked at an international bank. Every Friday, she brought home stamps from all the letters she had received during that week. I also had many penpals in different countries, and we wrote letters to each other very often. By the time I was twelve, I had collected more than 1000 stamps from 50 different countries! I've continued collecting stamps, but now it's more difficult. My mother retired from her job, and my penpals send me e-mail messages instead of letters. (The Internet has been very bad for my stamp collection!) Tell me, do you have a hobby? What do you enjoy doing in your free time? How long have you been doing that? Write and tell me about it.

Send a message to a keypal. Tell about your favorite hobby.

What Are They Saying?

9

Two-Word Verbs: Separable Inseparable

- Discussing When Things Are Going to Happen
- Remembering and Forgetting
- Discussing Obligations
- Asking for and Giving Advice
- School Assignments
- Making Plans by Telephone
- Talking About Important People in Your Life
- Shopping for Clothing

Vocabulary Preview

1. cross out
2. fill out
3. hand in
4. hang up
5. hook up
6. pick out
7. put away
8. put on
9. take down
10. take off
11. throw away
12. try on
13. turn on
14. turn off
15. wake up

Sometime Next Week

bring back the TV	**bring** it **back**
call up Sally	**call** her **up**
throw out the newspapers	**throw** them **out**

A. When is the repairman going to **bring back** our TV?

B. He's going to **bring** it **back** sometime next week.

1. When are you going to **call up** your uncle in Ohio?

2. When is Ted going to **throw out** his old newspapers?

3. When is your daughter going to **fill out** her college application forms?

4. When is Jeff going to **pick up** his clothes at the cleaner's?

5. When is Vicky going to **take back** her library books?

6. When are you going to **hook up** your new computer?

7. When is Howard going to **hang up** his new portrait?

8. When is Gloria going to **take down** her Christmas decorations?

9. When is Mr. Grumpkin going to **turn on** the heat in the building?

Oh, No! I Forgot!

put on your boots / put your boots **on** → put them **on**

A. Did you remember to { **turn off** the oven / **turn** the oven **off** } ?

B. Oh, no! I forgot! I'll **turn** it **off** right away.

1. *take back videos*

2. *fill out the accident report*

3. *turn on the alarm*

4. *put away your toys*

5. *hand in your English homework*

6. *wake up the kids*

7. *put on your raincoat*

8. *take off your boots*

9. *take out the garbage*

How to Say It!

Remembering & Forgetting

A. Did you remember to *turn off the oven*?

B. Oh, no! {
I forgot!
I forgot all about it!
I completely forgot!
It slipped my mind!
It completely slipped my mind!
}

Practice the conversations in this lesson again. Tell that you forgot in different ways.

READING

A BUSY SATURDAY

Everybody in the Peterson family is very busy today. It's Saturday, and they all have to do the things they didn't do during the week.

Mr. Peterson has to fill out his income tax form. He didn't have time to fill it out during the week.

Mrs. Peterson has to pick up her clothes at the cleaner's. She was too busy to pick them up during the week.

Their son Steve has to take his library books back. He forgot to take them back during the week.

Their other son, Michael, has to throw out all the old newspapers in the garage. He didn't have time to throw them out during the week.

Their daughter Stacey has to hook up the new modem for her computer. She was too busy to hook it up during the week.

And their other daughter, Abigail, has to put her toys away. She didn't feel like putting them away during the week.

As you can see, everybody in the Peterson family is going to be very busy today.

✓ READING *CHECK-UP*

Q & A

You're inviting somebody in the Peterson family to do something with you. Using this model, create dialogs based on the story.

A. Would you like to *play tennis* with me this morning?
B. I'd like to, but I can't. I have to *fill out my income tax form.*
A. That's too bad.
B. I know, but I've really got to do it. I *didn't have time to fill it out during the week.*
A. Well, maybe some other time.

How About You?

What do YOU have to do on your next day off from work or school?

I Don't Think So

A. Do you think I should keep these old love letters?

B. No, I don't think so. I think you should **throw** them **away**.

1. *hand in my homework*
   do over

2. *use up this old milk*
   throw out

3. *erase all my mistakes*
   cross out

4. *leave the air conditioner on*
   turn off

5. *try to remember Amy's telephone number*
   write down

6. *ask the teacher the definition of this word*
   look up

7. *make my decision right away*
   think over

8. *keep my ex-boyfriend's ring*
   give back

9. *accept this invitation to my ex-girlfriend's wedding*
   turn down

READING

LUCY'S ENGLISH COMPOSITION

Lucy is very discouraged. She handed in her English composition this morning, but her English teacher gave it back to her and told her to do it over. Apparently, her English teacher didn't like the way Lucy had done it. She hadn't erased her mistakes. She had simply crossed them out. Also, she had used several words incorrectly. She hadn't looked them up in a dictionary. And finally, she hadn't written her homework on the correct paper because she had accidentally thrown her notebook away. Poor Lucy! She didn't feel like writing her English composition in the first place, and now she has to do it over!

✓ READING *CHECK-UP*

TRUE, FALSE, OR MAYBE?

Answer True, False, or Maybe (if the answer isn't in the story).

1. Lucy gave her composition to her English teacher this morning.
2. Lucy's English teacher was satisfied with Lucy's composition.
3. The teacher gave back other students' compositions.
4. Lucy had made some mistakes in her composition.
5. Lucy knew the definitions of all the words she used in her composition.
6. Lucy is going to hand in her composition again tomorrow.

WHAT'S THE WORD?

Choose the correct words to complete the sentences.

cross ___ out	do ___ over	give ___ back	hand ___ in	look ___ up	throw ___ away

1. I need the dictionary you borrowed from me. Please ______.
2. I want to check your homework. Please ______.
3. Ms. Smith, there are too many mistakes in this letter. Please ______.
4. I haven't read today's newspaper yet. Please don't ______.
5. I don't remember his phone number. I've got to ______.
6. You should erase your mistakes. Don't just ______.

COMPLETE THE LETTERS

Complete these letters with the correct form of the verbs.

call ___ up   give ___ back   think ___ over   throw ___ away   turn ___ down

Dear Alice,

I'm very discouraged. I'm having a lot of trouble with my girlfriend, and I don't know what to do. The problem is very simple. I'm in love with her, but she isn't in love with me. A few weeks ago, I gave her a ring, but she _______1 to me. During the past few months, I have written several love letters to her, but she has _______2. Recently I asked her to marry me. She _______3 for a while, and then she _______4. Now when I try to _______5, she doesn't even want to talk to me. Please help me! I don't know what to do.

"Discouraged Donald"
Denver, Colorado

hang ___ up   put ___ away   take ___ down   take ___ out   turn ___ off   turn ___ on

Dear Alice,

I'm extremely frustrated. My husband is a very difficult person. Every time I do something, he does the opposite. For example, every time I turn on the stereo system to listen to music, he _______1. Every time I turn off the air conditioner in our apartment, he _______2. Last week I bought a beautiful new painting for our bedroom. The day after I _______3, he _______4. We had a lot of old photographs on a table in our living room. I decided to _______5 in a closet, but two hours later he _______6. Please help me! I don't know what to do.

"Frustrated Fran"
Phoenix, Arizona

What should "Discouraged Donald" and "Frustrated Fran" do? Write answers to their letters.

Would You Like to Get Together Today?

take back my library books = **take** my library books **back**

- **take** my library books **back**
- **pick up** my car at the repair shop
- **drop** my sister **off** at the airport

A. Would you like to get together today?

B. I'm afraid I can't. I have to **take** my library books **back**.

A. Are you free after you **take** them **back**?

B. I'm afraid not. I also have to **pick up** my car at the repair shop.

A. Would you like to get together after you **pick** it **up**?

B. I'd really like to, but I can't. I ALSO have to **drop** my sister **off** at the airport.

A. You're really busy today! What do you have to do after you **drop** her **off**?

B. Nothing. But by then I'll probably be exhausted. Let's get together tomorrow instead.

A. Fine. I'll call you in the morning.

A. Would you like to get together today?

B. I'm afraid I can't. I have to ________________.

A. Are you free after you ________________?

B. I'm afraid not. I also have to ________________.

A. Would you like to get together after you ________________?

B. I'd really like to, but I can't. I ALSO have to ________________.

A. You're really busy today! What do you have to do after you ________________?

B. Nothing. But by then I'll probably be exhausted. Let's get together tomorrow instead.

A. Fine. I'll call you in the morning.

☑ **clean up** my living room
☑ **throw out** all my old newspapers
☑ **pick** my brother **up** at the train station

1.

☑ **figure out** my hospital bill
☑ **fill out** my insurance form
☑ **call** the doctor **up**

2.

☑ **take down** my Christmas decorations
☑ **hang up** my New Year's decorations
☑ **drop** my suit **off** at the cleaner's

3.

☑ **pick out** my wedding dress
☑ **write down** the names of all the wedding guests
☑ **pick** the wedding invitations **up**

4.

☑ **clean up** my room
☑ **put** my toys **away**
☑ **do** my math homework **over**

5.

☑ ______________________________
☑ ______________________________
☑ ______________________________

6.

I Heard from Her Just Last Week

hear from Aunt Betty	**hear from** her
~~**hear** Aunt Betty **from**~~	~~**hear** her **from**~~

A. Have you **heard from** Aunt Betty recently?

B. Yes, I have. I **heard from** her just last week.

1. Have you **run into** Mr. Clark recently?

2. Have you **run out of** paper recently?

3. Has Martha **gotten over** the flu yet?

4. Has your English teacher **called on** you recently?

5. Have you and your husband **looked through** your photo album recently?

6. Has Ricky been **picking on** his little sister recently?

How About You?

Tell about some of the people in your life.

Do you have a good friend in another city? Who is he/she?
How often do you hear from him/her? How long have you known each other?
Who do you get along with very well? Why?
Who do you take after? How?
Who do you look up to? Why?

READING

A CHILD-REARING PROBLEM

Timothy and his little sister, Patty, don't get along with each other very well. In fact, they fight constantly. He picks on her when it's time for her to go to bed. She picks on him when his friends come over to play.

Timmy and Patty's parents are very concerned. They don't know what to do about their children. They have looked through several books on child rearing, but so far they can't seem to find an answer to the problem. They're hoping that eventually their children will learn to get along with each other better.

✓ READING *CHECK-UP*

TRUE, FALSE, OR MAYBE?

Answer True, False, or Maybe (if the answer isn't in the story).

1. Patty picks on Timmy when it's time for her go to bed.
2. Timmy is Patty's older brother.
3. Timmy and Patty's parents have a child-rearing problem.
4. They can't seem to find any books about child rearing.
5. Timmy and Patty will eventually learn to get along with each other better.

CHOOSE

1. Please don't _____ your little sister.
   a. pick on
   b. get along with
2. We've been _____ these old family pictures.
   a. looking through
   b. taking after
3. My history teacher _____ me three times today.
   a. looked up to
   b. called on
4. I haven't _____ my aunt and uncle recently.
   a. gotten over
   b. heard from
5. Everybody thinks I _____ my mother.
   a. take after
   b. look through
6. I really _____ my older sister because she's so smart.
   a. run into
   b. look up to
7. I _____ my cousin Jane on Main Street yesterday.
   a. ran into
   b. heard from
8. Don't kiss me! I haven't _____ my cold yet.
   a. gotten along with
   b. gotten over

ROLE PLAY *May I Help You?*

You're looking for clothing in a department store. Complete this conversation and act it out with another student.

A. May I help you?

B. Yes, please. I'm **looking for** (a/an) ________.

A. What size do you wear?

B. { Size 32/34/36/ . . .
Small/Medium/Large/Extra Large.

A. Here. How do you like (this one/these)?

B. Hmm. I think (it's/they're) a little too ________.* Do you have any ________s that are a little ________er?*

A. Yes. We have a wide selection. Why don't you **look through** all of our ________s and **pick out** the (one/ones) you like?

B. Can I **try** (it/them) **on**?

A. Of course. You can **try** (it/them) **on** in the dressing room over there.

* fancy – plain
dark – light

[5 minutes later]

A. Well, how (does it/do they) fit?

B. I'm afraid (it's/they're) a little too ________.* Do you have any ________s that are a little ________er*?

A. Yes, we do. I think you'll like (THIS/THESE) ________. (It's/They're) a little ________er* than the one(s) you just **tried on**.

B. Will you **take** (it/them) **back** if I decide to return (it/them)?

A. Of course. No problem at all. Just **bring** (it/them) **back** within ________ days, and we'll **give** you your money **back**.

B. Fine. I think I'll take (it/them). How much (does it/do they) cost?

A. The usual price is ________ dollars. But you're in luck! We're having a sale this week, and all of our ________s are ________ percent off the regular price.

B. That's a real bargain! I'm glad I decided to buy (a/an) ________ this week. Thanks for your help.

* large – small
long – short
wide – narrow
tight – loose (baggy)

1. *suit*

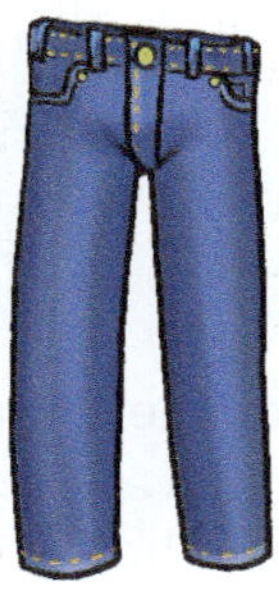

2. *jeans*

3. *sweater*

4.

How About You?

Where do you shop for clothing?
What kind of clothing do you like to wear?

Think about clothing you own:
- What's your favorite clothing item?
- How long have you had it?
- Where did you get it?
- Why is it your favorite?

ON SALE

Gary went to a men's clothing store yesterday. He was looking for a new sports jacket. He looked through the entire selection of jackets and picked out a few that he really liked. First, he picked out a nice blue jacket. But when he tried it on, it was too small. Next, he picked out an attractive red jacket. But when he tried it on, it was too large. Finally, he picked out a very fancy brown jacket with gold buttons. And when he tried it on, it seemed to fit perfectly.

Then he decided to buy a pair of trousers to go with the jacket. He looked through the entire selection of trousers and picked out several pairs that he really liked. First, he picked out a light brown pair. But when he tried them on, they were too tight. Next, he tried on a dark brown pair. But when he tried them on, they were too loose. Finally, he picked out a pair of brown-and-white plaid pants. And when he tried them on, they seemed to fit perfectly.

Gary paid for his new clothing and walked home feeling very happy about the jacket and pants he had just bought. He was especially happy because the clothing was on sale, and he had paid fifty percent off the regular price. However, Gary's happiness didn't last very long. When he got home, he noticed that one arm of the jacket was longer than the other. He also realized very quickly that the zipper on the pants was broken.

The next day Gary took the clothing back to the store and tried to get a refund. However, the people at the store refused to give him his money back because the clothing was on sale and there was a sign that said "All Sales Are Final!" Gary was furious, but he knew he couldn't do anything about it. The next time he buys something on sale, he'll be more careful. And he'll be sure to read the signs!

READING *CHECK-UP*

WHAT'S THE SEQUENCE?

Put these events in the correct order, based on the story.

____ Gary picked out a few jackets he really liked.
____ Gary went back and asked for a refund.
__1__ Gary went shopping for clothes yesterday.
____ He walked home feeling very happy.
____ He walked home feeling very upset and angry.
____ The brown jacket seemed to fit perfectly.
____ The store refused to give him back his money.
____ A pair of plaid pants fit very well.
____ He paid only half of the regular price.
____ He picked out several pairs of trousers.
____ But then, Gary noticed a few problems with the jacket and the pants.

How About You?

Have you ever bought something you had to return?
- What did you buy?
- Where?
- What was wrong with it?
- What did you do?
- Were you successful?

LISTENING

Listen and choose what the people are talking about.

1. a. shorts
   b. a blouse
2. a. shoes
   b. a library book
3. a. an application form
   b. a math problem
4. a. homework
   b. children
5. a. pictures
   b. pants
6. a. the flu
   b. a decision
7. a. a coat
   b. the heat
8. a. milk
   b. the garbage
9. a. a telephone number
   b. an invitation

PRONUNCIATION Linking "t" Between Vowels

Listen. Then say it.

Turn it on!

Turn it off!

Clean it up!

Throw it away!

Say it. Then listen.

Fill it out!

Do it over!

Drop it off!

Hand it in!

Write in your journal about someone you look up to—a member of your family, a person in your community, or a famous person in your country or in history. Who do you look up to? Why do you admire this person?

GRAMMAR FOCUS

Two-Word Verbs: Separable

I'm going to	**put on** my boots. **put** my boots **on**. **put** them **on**.

Two-Word Verbs: Inseparable

I	**hear from** Aunt Betty **hear from** her ~~hear Aunt Betty from~~ ~~hear her from~~	very often.

Complete the sentences.

1. A. When are you going to throw out those old magazines?
   B. I'll _____ _____ _____ this weekend.
2. A. Have you heard from your cousins in Detroit recently?
   B. Yes, I have. I _____ _____ _____ a few weeks ago.
3. A. Did you hook up your new computer?
   B. Not yet. I'm going to _____ _____ _____ tonight.
4. A. Did you fill out the insurance form?
   B. Oh, no! I forgot. I'll _____ _____ _____ right away.
5. A. Does your English teacher call on you a lot in class?
   B. Yes. She _____ _____ _____ all the time.
6. A. I hope you get over the flu soon.
   B. I'm sure I'll _____ _____ _____ in a few days.
7. A. Please take out the garbage!
   B. I _____ _____ _____ a few minutes ago.
8. A. Lilly, did you put away your toys?
   B. Yes, I did. I _____ _____ _____ a little while ago.
9. A. Have you run into your old friend Bob recently?
   B. Yes, I have. I _____ _____ _____ just the other day.
10. A. How do you get along with your neighbors?
    B. I _____ _____ _____ _____ very well.
11. A. Don't forget to take back the videos.
    B. Don't worry. I'll _____ _____ _____ today.

10

Connectors: And . . . Too And . . . Either So, But, Neither

- Coincidences
- Asking for and Giving Reasons
- Describing People's Backgrounds, Interests, and Personalities
- Looking for a Job
- Referring People to Someone Else
- Discussing Opinions
- Describing People's Similarities and Differences

VOCABULARY PREVIEW

1. allergic
2. athletic
3. frightened
4. strict
5. lenient
6. alarm clock
7. army
8. lightning
9. parking space
10. want ad
11. enroll
12. hide
13. kiss
14. walk *my* dog
15. work out

What a Coincidence!

I'm hungry.	I am, too. / So am I.	I have a car.	I do, too. / So do I.
I can swim.	I can, too. / So can I.	I worked yesterday.	I did, too. / So did I.
I've seen that movie.	I have, too. / So have I.		

A. I'm allergic to cats.

B. What a coincidence!
{ I am, too. / So am I. }

1. I'm a vegetarian.

2. I like peppermint ice cream.

3. I can speak four languages fluently.

4. I just got a raise.

5. I'll be on a business trip next week.

6. I've been feeling tired lately.

7. I have to work late at the office tonight.

8. I forgot my umbrella this morning.

9.

What a Coincidence!

I'm not hungry.	I'm not either. / Neither am I.	I don't have a car.	I don't either. / Neither do I.
I can't swim.	I can't either. / Neither can I.	I didn't work yesterday.	I didn't either. / Neither did I.
I haven't seen that movie.	I haven't either. / Neither have I.		

A. I'm not a very good dancer.

B. What a coincidence!
{ I'm not either. / Neither am I. }

1. I don't like macaroni and cheese.

2. I didn't see the stop sign.

3. I can't skate very well.

4. I haven't seen a movie in a long time.

5. I wasn't very athletic when I was younger.

6. I won't be able to go bowling next Saturday.

7. I don't have a date for the prom.

8. I've never kissed anyone before.

9.

And They Do, Too

I'm tired, { and he is, too. / and so is he. }	They sing, { and she does, too. / and so does she. }
He'll be busy, { and she will, too. / and so will she. }	She studied, { and I did, too. / and so did I. }
She's been sick, { and he has, too. / and so has he. }	

A. Why can't you or the children help me with the dishes?

B. I have to study, { **and they do, too.** / **and so do they.** }

1. Why weren't you and Bob at the meeting this morning?
I missed the bus, _____.

2. Why are you and Vanessa so nervous today?
I have two final exams tomorrow, _____.

3. What are you and your brother going to do when you grow up?
I'm going to start an Internet company, _____.

4. Where were you and your wife when the accident happened?
I was standing on the corner, _____.

5. How do you know Mr. and Mrs. Crandall?
They walk their dog in the park, ____.

6. Why can't you or your roommates come to my party?
I'll be out of town, ____.

7. Why haven't you and your brother been in school for the past few days?
I've been sick, ____.

8. Could you or your friend help me take these packages upstairs?
I'll be glad to help you, ____.

9. How did you meet your wife?
I was working out at the health club, ____.

10. What are you two arguing about?
He wants this parking space, ____.

11. Why don't you or your neighbors complain about this leak?
I've already spoken to the landlord, ____.

12. How did you and your husband like the play?
I fell asleep during the first act, ____.

13. Why are you and your cats hiding under the bed?
I'm afraid of thunder and lightning, ____.

14.

READING

"MADE FOR EACH OTHER"

Louise and Brian are very compatible people. They have a lot in common. For example, they have similar backgrounds. He grew up in a small town in the South, and so did she. She's the oldest of four children, and he is, too. His parents own their own business, and so do hers.

They also have similar academic interests. She's majoring in chemistry, and he is, too. He has taken every course in mathematics offered by their college, and so has she. She enjoys working with computers, and he does, too.

In addition, Louise and Brian like the same sports. He goes swimming several times a week, and so does she. She can play tennis very well, and so can he. His favorite winter sport is ice skating, and hers is, too.

Louise and Brian also have the same cultural interests. She has been to most of the art museums in New York City, and so has he. He's a member of the college theater group, and she is, too. She has a complete collection of Beethoven's symphonies, and so does he.

In addition, they have similar personalities. She has always been very shy, and he has, too. He tends to be very quiet, and so does she. She's often nervous when she's in large groups of people, and he is, too.

Finally, they have very similar outlooks on life. She has been a vegetarian for years, and so has he. He supports equal rights for women and minorities, and so does she. She's opposed to the use of nuclear energy, and he is, too.

As you can see, Louise and Brian are very compatible people. In fact, everybody says they were "made for each other."

✓ READING *CHECK-UP*

TRUE, FALSE, OR MAYBE?

Answer True, False, or Maybe (if the answer isn't in the story).

1. Louise spent her childhood in the South.
2. Brian has older brothers and sisters.
3. Louise and Brian are both students in college.
4. They both ski very well.
5. They haven't been to all the art museums in New York City.
6. They both like to be in large groups of people.
7. They both feel that people shouldn't eat vegetables.

LISTENING

Listen and choose what the people are talking about.

1. a. personality
   b. background
2. a. sports
   b. cultural interests
3. a. academic interests
   b. outlook on life
4. a. personality
   b. background
5. a. sports
   b. academic interests
6. a. cultural interests
   b. outlook on life

And She Hasn't Either

I'm not tired, { and he isn't either. / and neither is he. }	They don't sing, { and she doesn't either. / and neither does she. }
He won't be busy, { and she won't either. / and neither will she. }	She didn't study, { and I didn't either. / and neither did I. }
She hasn't been sick, { and he hasn't either. / and neither has he. }	

A. Why do you and your sister look so frightened?

B. I've never been on a roller coaster before, { **and she hasn't either.** / **and neither has she.** }

1. Why haven't you and your roommate hooked up your new DVD player?
   I don't understand the instructions, ____.

2. Why didn't you or your parents answer the telephone all weekend?
   I wasn't home, ____.

3. Why did you and your wife move to the center of the city?
   She didn't like living in the suburbs, ____.

4. What do you and Greg want to talk to me about?
   I won't be able to work overtime this weekend, ____.

5. Why do you and your husband want to enroll in my dance class?
I don't know how to dance, ____.

6. Why does the school nurse want to see us?
I haven't had an eye examination, ____.

7. Why didn't you or Mom wake us up on time this morning?
I didn't hear the alarm clock, ____.

8. Why did you and your husband leave the concert so early?
I couldn't stand the loud music, ____.

9. What are you and your sister arguing about?
She doesn't want to take the garbage out, ____.

10. Why don't you and your friends want to come to the game?
They aren't very interested in football, ____.

11. Why were you and your wife so nervous during the flight?
I had never flown before today, ____.

12. Why have you and your friends stopped shopping at my store?
I can't afford your prices, ____.

13. Why don't you and your sister want me to read "Little Red Riding Hood"?
I don't like fairy tales very much, ____.

14.

READING

LAID OFF

Jack and Betty Williams are going through some difficult times. They were both laid off from their jobs last month. As the days go by, they're becoming more and more concerned about their futures, since he hasn't been able to find another job yet, and neither has she.

The layoffs weren't a surprise to Jack and Betty. After all, Jack's company hadn't been doing very well for a long time, and neither had Betty's. However, Jack had never expected both of them to be laid off at the same time, and Betty hadn't either. Ever since they have been laid off, Jack and Betty have been trying to find new jobs. Unfortunately, she hasn't been very successful, and he hasn't either.

The main reason they're having trouble finding work is that there simply aren't many jobs available right now. He can't find anything in the want ads, and neither can she. She hasn't heard about any job openings, and he hasn't either. His friends haven't been able to help at all, and neither have hers.

Another reason they're having trouble finding work is that they don't seem to have the right kind of skills and training. He doesn't know anything about computers, and she doesn't either. She can't type very well, and neither can he. He hasn't had any special vocational training, and she hasn't either.

A third reason they're having trouble finding work is that there are certain jobs they prefer not to take. He doesn't like working at night, and neither does she. She isn't willing to work on the weekends, and neither is he. He doesn't want to commute very far to work, and she doesn't either.

Despite all their problems, Jack and Betty aren't completely discouraged. She doesn't have a very pessimistic outlook on life, and neither does he. They're both hopeful that things will get better soon.

✓ READING *CHECK-UP*

TRUE, FALSE, OR MAYBE?

Answer True, False, or Maybe (if the answer isn't in the story).

1. Betty quit her job last month.
2. Jack and Betty had been working for the same company.
3. Some of their friends have been laid off, too.
4. Typing skills are important in certain jobs.
5. Jack and Betty will find jobs soon.

You're at a job interview. Role-play with another student, using the interviewer's questions below.

Tell me about your skills.
Tell me about your educational background.
Have you had any special vocational training?
Are you willing to work at night or on the weekend?
When can you start?

You Should Ask Them

I don't sing, **but** my sister does.	He can play chess, **but** I can't.
She didn't know the answer, **but** I did.	We're ready, **but** they aren't.

A. Can you baby-sit for us tomorrow night?

B. No, I can't, but my SISTER can. You should ask HER.

1. Have you heard the weather forecast?
   my father

2. Do you have a hammer?
   my upstairs neighbors

3. Are you interested in seeing a movie tonight?
   Maria

4. Did you write down the homework assignment?
   Jack

5. Have you by any chance found a brown-and-white dog?
   the woman across the street

6. Were you paying attention when the salesman explained how to assemble this?
   the children

How to Say It!

Offering a Suggestion

Practice the conversations in this lesson again. Offer suggestions in different ways.

READING

"TOUCHY SUBJECTS"

Larry and his parents always disagree when they talk about politics. Larry is very liberal, but his parents aren't. They're very conservative. Larry thinks the president is doing a very poor job, but his parents don't. They think the president is doing a fine job. Also, Larry doesn't think the government should spend a lot of money on defense, but his parents do. They think the country needs a strong army. You can see why Larry and his parents always disagree when they talk about politics. Politics is a very "touchy subject" with them.

The Greens and their next-door neighbors, the Harrisons, always disagree when they talk about child rearing. The Greens are very lenient with their children, but the Harrisons aren't. They're very strict. The Greens let their children watch television whenever they want, but the Harrisons don't. They let their children watch television for only an hour a day. Also, the Harrisons have always taught their children to sit quietly and behave well at the dinner table, but the Greens haven't. They have always allowed their children to do whatever they want at the dinner table. You can see why the Greens and the Harrisons always disagree when they talk about child rearing. Child rearing is a very "touchy subject" with them.

✓ READING *CHECK-UP*

TRUE, FALSE, OR MAYBE?

Answer True, False, or Maybe (if the answer isn't in the story).

1. Larry and his parents never agree when they talk about politics.
2. Larry probably supports equal rights for women and minorities.
3. The Harrisons' children watch television more often than the Greens' children.
4. The Greens' children probably go to bed later than the Harrisons' children.
5. Since the Greens and the Harrisons disagree, they never talk about child rearing.

How About You?

Do you and someone you know always disagree about a "touchy subject"? Who is this person? What do you disagree about? In what ways do you disagree?

ON YOUR OWN *Same and Different*

In many ways, my sister and I are exactly the same.
I'm tall and thin, and she is, too.
I have brown eyes and curly black hair, and so does she.
I work in an office downtown, and she does, too.
I'm not married yet, and neither is she.
I went to college in Boston, and so did she.
I wasn't a very good student, and she wasn't either.

And in many ways, my sister and I are very different.
I like classical music, but she doesn't.
She enjoys sports, but I don't.
I've never traveled overseas, but she has.
She's never been to New York, but I have many times.
She's very outgoing and popular, but I'm not.
I'm very quiet and philosophical, but she isn't.

Yes, in many ways, my sister and I are exactly the same, and in many ways, we're very different. But most important of all, we like and respect each other. And we're friends.

Tell other students about somebody you are close to—a friend, a classmate, or someone in your family. Tell how you and this person are the same, and tell how you are different.

SIDE by SIDE JOURNAL

Write in your journal about somebody you are close to—a friend, a classmate, or someone in your family. Tell how you and this person are the same, and tell how you are different.

In many ways, ____________ and I are exactly the same.

____

____

____

And in many ways, ____________ and I are very different.

____

____

____

PRONUNCIATION Contrastive Stress

Listen. Then say it.

No, I can't, but my SISTER can.

No, I don't, but my NEIGHBORS do.

You should ask HER.

Why don't you ask THEM?

Say it. Then listen.

No, I haven't, but my FATHER has.

No, I wasn't, but my CHILDREN were.

You should ask HIM.

How about asking THEM?

GRAMMAR FOCUS

CONNECTORS:

TOO/SO

I'm hungry.	I am, too. So am I.
I can swim.	I can, too. So can I.
I've seen that movie.	I have, too. So have I.
I have a car.	I do, too. So do I.
I worked yesterday.	I did, too. So did I.

EITHER/NEITHER

I'm not hungry.	I'm not either. Neither am I.
I can't swim.	I can't either. Neither can I.
I've haven't seen that movie.	I haven't either. Neither have I.
I don't have a car.	I don't either. Neither do I.
I didn't work.	I didn't either. Neither did I.

BUT

I don't sing, **but** my sister does.

She didn't know the answer, **but** I did.

He can play chess, **but** I can't.

We're ready, **but** they aren't.

I'm tired,	and he is, too. and so is he.
He'll be busy,	and she will, too. and so will she.
She's been sick,	and he has, too. and so has he.
They sing,	and she does, too. and so does she.
She studied,	and I did, too. and so did I.

I'm not tired,	and he isn't either. and neither is he.
He won't be busy,	and she won't either. and neither will she.
She hasn't been sick,	and he hasn't either. and neither has he.
They don't sing,	and she doesn't either. and neither does she.
She didn't study,	and I didn't either. and neither did I.

Complete the sentences.

1. She just got a raise, and _____ _____ I.
2. He hasn't arrived yet, and _____ _____ they.
3. They can't lift it, and we _____ _____.
4. I have to work late, and you _____, _____.
5. She's leaving soon, and _____ _____ we.
6. He doesn't like to swim, and I _____ _____.
7. A. Are you interested in sports?
   B. No, _____ _____, but my sister _____.
8. I'm going to a meeting, and they _____, _____.
9. He hadn't been there before, and she _____ _____.
10. I won't be able to go, and _____ _____ you.
11. She types very well, and he _____, _____.
12. We've been very busy, and _____ _____ she.
13. You aren't allergic to anything, and _____ _____ I.
14. A. Do you have a ladder?
    B. No, I _____, but my neighbor _____.

SIDE by SIDE Gazette

Volume 3 Number 4

From Matchmakers to Dating Services

Traditions, customs, modern life, and the ways people meet

Marriage traditions and customs are very different around the world. In many cultures, young people meet at school, at work, or in other places; they decide to go out together; they fall in love; and they get married. In other cultures, parents or other family members arrange a match between two young people.

In India, for example, a father traditionally finds his daughter a husband. The father might ask friends or relatives to recommend a possible husband, and he might put an ad in the newspaper. The father looks for someone with a good education, occupation, and salary. When he finds a possible match, he sends his daughter's horoscope to the boy's family. An astrologer reads the horoscope and decides if there is a good astrological match between the young man and woman. If the astrologer approves, the families then discuss the marriage arrangements.

In many cultures around the world, families use a matchmaker to bring young people together and arrange marriages. This is especially common in rural areas of many countries. Families pay the matchmaker to find a partner for their child. Sometimes, the matchmaker also helps families with the "business" part of a marriage agreement. For example, a family may give or receive animals, products, or other valuable things as part of the marriage arrangement. In some cultures, parents even arrange marriages between children before they are born.

An astrologer approved the marriage of these newlyweds from India. The astrologer examined their horoscopes to decide if the date and time of their births were a good match.

These traditions and customs are changing in many places, especially in the modern cities of the world. Young people want the freedom to choose their own partners. Many, however, actually use modern-day versions of the traditional matchmaking services! For example, some people put personal ads in newspapers or magazines. In these ads, people describe themselves and tell what kind of person they're looking for. Others use dating services—companies that bring people together. Most dating services ask people to submit a photograph and fill out a long questionnaire about their background and interests. Some dating services even make videos of their customers. People who use a dating service can usually browse through the company's information to find a possible partner.

FACT FILE

When People Get Married

People around the world get married at different ages. At what age do men and women usually get married in different countries you know?

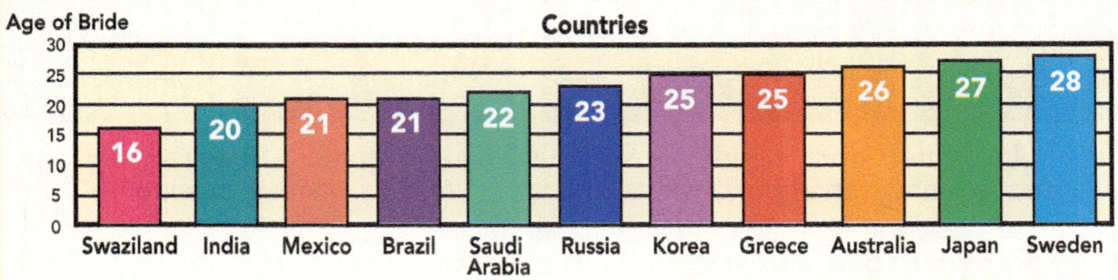

AROUND THE WORLD

Wedding Customs and Traditions

a wedding ceremony in the United States

a Hindu ceremony

a wedding in the Slovak Republic

a ceremony in a Korean village

Wedding customs and traditions are very different around the world. In many cultures, weddings happen in churches or other places of worship. In other cultures, people get married outdoors, in their homes, in special reception halls for family celebrations, or in other places. The bride and the groom usually wear clothing that is traditional for weddings in their culture. The type of clothing and the colors are very different around the world. Brides often wear a veil or a crown on their heads. Some weddings are private—just for family members and friends. Other weddings are public. Everybody in the neighborhood or the entire town might attend the celebration. Some weddings are short, and other weddings can last for hours, days, or even a week!

a traditional Romanian dance

musicians leading a wedding procession

Music and dancing are an important part of wedding celebrations in different cultures. There are often special dances for the bride and groom, their parents, and other family members. Musicians might play special wedding music during the ceremony, at the celebration after the ceremony, or even in the street!

confetti

flower petals

rice

In some cultures, people like to throw things at weddings! Before or after the ceremony, it is often traditional for guests to shower the bride and groom with something to wish them good luck.

Guests have pinned money on this bride and groom in Cyprus.

a wedding couple in Colombia lighting candles during the ceremony

cutting the cake at a U.S. wedding celebration

a Japanese bride arriving at her wedding by boat

a bride in the U.S. throwing a bouquet of flowers (According to tradition, the person who catches it will get married next.)

Many cultures around the world have special wedding customs. These traditions often involve candles, flowers, special foods, money, and the ways that couples get to their wedding ceremonies.

What wedding customs and traditions in different cultures do you know?

Interview

A* Side by Side Gazette *reporter spoke with several young couples.

Q: "How did you meet?"

A: We met in college.

A: We met at work.

A: We met at a bookstore.

A: We were high school "sweethearts."

A: We met on a "blind date" that our friends arranged.

A: We met through a dating service.

A: Our parents arranged our marriage through a matchmaker.

FUN with IDIOMS

Do You Know These Expressions?

_____ 1. He's nuts about me.

_____ 2. She gave me the cold shoulder.

_____ 3. I fell for him the moment I met him.

_____ 4. We had planned to go on a date, but she stood me up.

a. I liked him right away.

b. He likes me a lot.

c. She didn't meet me.

d. She didn't pay attention to me.

We've Got Mail!

Dear Side by Side,

I'm trying to figure out two-word verbs. Is there a rule that will tell me which two-word verbs are separable and which are inseparable? I hope to hear you from soon.

Sincerely,

"Looking for an Answer"

Dear "Looking for an Answer,"

We're sorry to tell you that there isn't a rule for this. You need to learn about each verb separately. Here's a suggestion. On a piece of paper, make two lists. Write down separable two-word verbs in one list and inseparable two-word verbs in the other. Then look up the words on your lists when you can't remember them.

By the way, we've circled some words in the last sentence of your letter because "hear from" is an inseparable two-word verb. The correct way to say this is "I hope to hear from you soon." Thanks for writing, and good luck with two-word verbs!

Sincerely,

Side by Side

Dear Side by Side,

I think two-word verbs are very difficult. The verb in a two-word verb has one meaning, but the whole two-word verb often has a different meaning. For example, "I turned on the light," but "I turned down the invitation"; "I take out the garbage," but "I take after my father." In my language, we have different words for all these expressions. Why does English use the same words over and over again?

Sincerely,

"Turned Off by Two-Word Verbs"

Dear "Turned Off,"

We're sorry to hear you're unhappy. Two-word verbs are very common in everyday English. We actually have special words for many of these meanings, but these words are more formal. For example, you can say, "I declined the invitation" and "I resemble my father." Most English speakers, however, prefer to use informal language, so they use lots of two-word verbs. With time, we're sure you'll get over this problem with two-word verbs. Thanks for your question.

Sincerely,

Side by Side

Global Exchange

PedroJ: Let me tell you about my best friend. His name is Marco. People think we're brothers because we look alike. He's short and thin, and so am I. I have curly brown hair, and he does, too. We also have similar backgrounds. He's originally from Peru, and I am, too. He moved to this country when he was a little boy, and so did I. His parents work in factories, and so do mine. Marco and I have very different interests. He enjoys playing sports, but I don't. I play a musical instrument, but he doesn't. I've been in several plays in school, but he hasn't. How about you? Tell me about your best friend.

Tell a keypal about your best friend.

LISTENING

"Telephone Tag" True or False?

____ 1 Mary likes jazz, and Jim does, too.

____ 2 Mary likes to play tennis, and so does Jim.

____ 3 Jim wants to go to the ballet, but Mary doesn't.

____ 4 Jim hasn't seen the movie, and neither has Mary.

____ 5 Jim doesn't like Italian food, but Mary does.

What Are They Saying?

CHECK-UP TESTS
SKILLS CHECKS

CHAPTER 1 • Check-up Test • Skills Check

Choose the correct answer.

1. My grandmother is knitting ____.
   (A) cookies
   (B) dinner
   (C) a sweater
   (D) her car

2. Roger is very talented. He composes ____.
   (A) paintings
   (B) music
   (C) the violin
   (D) computers

3. I'm ironing ____.
   (A) my bicycle
   (B) my son
   (C) the kitchen
   (D) these pants

4. My daughter ____ soccer every day after school
   (A) practices
   (B) exercises
   (C) acts
   (D) goes

5. Marisa plays several sports. She's a very good ____.
   (A) artist
   (B) actress
   (C) athlete
   (D) driver

6. ____ TV very often, but ____ TV today.
   (A) I watch . . . I'm watching
   (B) I'm not watching . . . I watch
   (C) I'm watching . . . I don't watch
   (D) I don't watch . . . I'm watching

7. Max ____ ski. ____ very good skier.
   (A) doesn't like . . . Isn't he a
   (B) likes to . . . He's
   (C) doesn't like to . . . He isn't a
   (D) isn't liking to . . . He isn't

8. I'm ____ English. What ____?
   (A) studying . . . you are studying
   (B) study . . . do you study
   (C) studying . . . are you studying
   (D) studying . . . are you're studying

9. A. What ____ talking about?
   B. ____ about their jobs.
   (A) they're . . . They're talking
   (B) are they . . . They're talking
   (C) are they . . . Their talking
   (D) they . . . They talking

10. A. How often ____?
    B. ____ every weekend.
    (A) do they call you . . . They call me
    (B) they call you . . . They call me
    (C) are they calling you . . . They calling
    (D) they calling you . . . They're calling me

SKILLS CHECK

Match the "can do" statement and the correct sentence.

____	1. I can ask about current activities.	a. Do you like to dance?
____	2. I can tell about current activities.	b. She's an excellent tennis player.
____	3. I can ask about likes.	c. Oh, really?
____	4. I can ask about frequency of actions.	d. I'm studying.
____	5. I can tell about frequency of actions.	e. How often do you call her?
____	6. I can react to information.	f. I want to be a professional soccer player.
____	7. I can tell about skills.	g. I call her every Sunday evening.
____	8. I can tell about my goals.	h. What are you doing?

Choose the correct answer.

1. He _____ and fell while he was getting out of a taxi.
   Ⓐ ripped
   Ⓑ tripped
   Ⓒ taught
   Ⓓ took

2. I sprained my _____ while I was jogging through the park.
   Ⓐ ankle
   Ⓑ uncle
   Ⓒ pants
   Ⓓ wallet

3. I'm really upset. I _____ my cell phone yesterday.
   Ⓐ met
   Ⓑ slept
   Ⓒ hiked
   Ⓓ lost

4. I fell asleep during my history class because I was _____.
   Ⓐ prepared
   Ⓑ scared
   Ⓒ bored
   Ⓓ embarrassed

5. We _____ the city by taxi.
   Ⓐ got
   Ⓑ got around
   Ⓒ took
   Ⓓ went

6. We _____ our dinner because the food _____ very good.
   Ⓐ didn't like . . . wasn't
   Ⓑ didn't liked . . . was
   Ⓒ didn't like . . . didn't be
   Ⓓ didn't liked . . . wasn't

7. Carla _____ the train to work today. She _____ the bus.
   Ⓐ didn't take . . . taked
   Ⓑ didn't took . . . tooked
   Ⓒ took . . . didn't taked
   Ⓓ took . . . didn't take

8. Dave _____ his arm while he _____ tennis.
   Ⓐ was breaking . . . played
   Ⓑ broke . . . was playing
   Ⓒ was broking . . . was playing
   Ⓓ breaked . . . played

9. A. What _____ last weekend?
   B. I _____ to the beach.
   Ⓐ did you do . . . went
   Ⓑ did you did . . . did go
   Ⓒ you did do . . . went
   Ⓓ you was doing . . . was going

10. A. How _____ home from their trip?
    B. They _____ home by boat.
    Ⓐ did they come . . . comed
    Ⓑ they came . . . came
    Ⓒ they did came . . . camed
    Ⓓ did they come . . . came

SKILLS CHECK

Match the "can do" statement and the correct sentence.

_____	**1.** I can ask about past activities.	**a.** I was sad.
_____	**2.** I can tell about my past activities.	**b.** She sprained her ankle.
_____	**3.** I can describe my feelings and emotions.	**c.** You know . . .
_____	**4.** I can describe a mishap.	**d.** What did you do yesterday?
_____	**5.** I can ask about how something happened.	**e.** How did he lose his wallet?
_____	**6.** I can react to bad news.	**f.** That's a shame!
_____	**7.** I can start a conversation.	**g.** I painted my apartment.

CHAPTER 3

- Check-up Test
- Skills Check

Choose the correct answer.

1. Mrs. Tanaka is at a meeting. She'll ____ in a little while.
   - Ⓐ return
   - Ⓑ receive
   - Ⓒ require
   - Ⓓ realize

2. My wife and I will be ____ our income tax returns tonight.
   - Ⓐ writing
   - Ⓑ paying
   - Ⓒ filling out
   - Ⓓ working out

3. I'll be very happy to ____ you my screwdriver.
   - Ⓐ take
   - Ⓑ browse
   - Ⓒ borrow
   - Ⓓ lend

4. My brother and I will be ____ a wedding in Cleveland this weekend.
   - Ⓐ arriving
   - Ⓑ attending
   - Ⓒ assembling
   - Ⓓ adjusting

5. I'm really ____ my vacation at the beach next month.
   - Ⓐ looking for
   - Ⓑ looking like
   - Ⓒ looking forward to
   - Ⓓ liking

6. ____ a movie this weekend. ____ a movie last weekend.
   - Ⓐ I'm going to see . . . I didn't saw
   - Ⓑ I'm not going to see . . . I saw
   - Ⓒ I'll be see . . . I didn't see
   - Ⓓ I saw . . . I'm going to see

7. The plane ____ arrive ____ 9:45 P.M.
   - Ⓐ will . . . until
   - Ⓑ won't . . . for
   - Ⓒ won't . . . until
   - Ⓓ will . . . in

8. ____ be home. ____ all evening.
   - Ⓐ I won't . . . I attend a meeting
   - Ⓑ We'll . . . We'll be reading
   - Ⓒ She won't . . . She'll working
   - Ⓓ He'll . . . He'll be watch TV

9. I'm sorry I can't lend you my ladder. ____ is broken. But I'm sure my brother will be happy to lend you ____. Call and ask ____.
   - Ⓐ It's . . . its . . . it
   - Ⓑ Ours . . . our . . . us
   - Ⓒ My . . . mine . . . them
   - Ⓓ Mine . . . his . . . him

10. We're moving to a different city. ____ in a few minutes. We're sad because we ____ our family and friends for a long time.
    - Ⓐ We'll be leaving . . . won't be seeing
    - Ⓑ We'll be leave . . . will be seeing
    - Ⓒ We're going to leaving . . . will see
    - Ⓓ Will be leaving . . . won't going to see

SKILLS CHECK

Match the "can do" statement and the correct sentence.

____	1. I can ask about future plans.	a.	The play will begin at 7:30.
____	2. I can tell about future plans.	b.	How much longer will you be doing homework?
____	3. I can ask about the time of an event.	c.	Could you do me a favor?
____	4. I can tell about the time of an event.	d.	I'm going to make pea soup.
____	5. I can ask about the duration of an event.	e.	Hi, Carla. This is Maria.
____	6. I can tell about the duration of an event.	f.	What are you going to do this weekend?
____	7. I can call someone.	g.	I'll be ironing for another five minutes.
____	8. I can ask a favor.	h.	Will the train arrive soon?

Choose the correct answer.

1. Samantha got a raise, and now her _____ is higher.
   Ⓐ report
   Ⓑ elevator
   Ⓒ boss
   Ⓓ salary

2. I went to the doctor for an examination. She gave me _____.
   Ⓐ a presentation
   Ⓑ the flu
   Ⓒ an injection
   Ⓓ X-rays

3. Would you like to go _____ on the river this weekend?
   Ⓐ kayaking
   Ⓑ camping
   Ⓒ hiking
   Ⓓ bowling

4. Did you watch the president's _____ about world problems on television last night?
   Ⓐ course
   Ⓑ speech
   Ⓒ inventory
   Ⓓ term paper

5. I didn't understand the present perfect tense, but my teacher _____ it very well.
   Ⓐ examined
   Ⓑ complained
   Ⓒ explained
   Ⓓ expressed

6. A. _____ in a helicopter the other day.
   B. Really? _____ in a helicopter.
   Ⓐ I flown . . . I never flew
   Ⓑ I flew . . . I've never flew
   Ⓒ I flew . . . I've never flown
   Ⓓ I've flown . . . I never flew

7. A. _____ with your supervisor yet?
   B. Yes. _____ with her a little while ago.
   Ⓐ Did you speak . . . I spoken
   Ⓑ Have you spoken . . . I spoke
   Ⓒ Did you spoke . . . I've spoken
   Ⓓ Have you spoke . . . I spoke

8. My parents like to go dancing. But _____ dancing for a long time.
   Ⓐ they didn't go
   Ⓑ they haven't went
   Ⓒ they've gone
   Ⓓ they haven't gone

9. A. _____ your medicine yet?
   B. _____. I have to take it in an hour.
   Ⓐ Did you taken . . . Yes, I have
   Ⓑ Have you take . . . No, haven't
   Ⓒ Have you taken . . . No, I haven't
   Ⓓ Did you take . . . Yes, I did

10. _____ a wonderful play recently. It's one of the best plays _____.
   Ⓐ I saw . . . I've ever seen
   Ⓑ I've seen . . . I've ever saw
   Ⓒ I seen . . . I ever saw
   Ⓓ I've saw . . . I ever see

SKILLS CHECK

Match the "can do" statement and the correct sentence.

_____ 1. I can ask about a person's skills.
_____ 2. I can describe my work experience.
_____ 3. I can describe actions that have already occurred.
_____ 4. I can describe actions that haven't occurred yet.
_____ 5. I can ask about likes.
_____ 6. I can react to information.
_____ 7. I can ask about past activities.
_____ 8. I can express satisfaction.

a. Do you like to draw?
b. Do you know how to drive trucks?
c. What movie did you see?
d. I've already done my laundry this week.
e. It's one of the best books I've ever read.
f. I've taken X-rays for many years.
g. Really?
h. I've never ridden in a limousine.

Choose the correct answer.

1. Ahmed called his doctor because he felt ____.
   Ⓐ engaged
   Ⓑ busy
   Ⓒ dizzy
   Ⓓ full

2. My wife and I are very upset. Our house has ____.
   Ⓐ termites
   Ⓑ satellites
   Ⓒ measles
   Ⓓ a high fever

3. Someday I want to ____ my own business.
   Ⓐ know
   Ⓑ own
   Ⓒ count
   Ⓓ wait for

4. Ben comes to work early and leaves late. He's a very dedicated ____.
   Ⓐ patient
   Ⓑ teenager
   Ⓒ store manager
   Ⓓ bachelor

5. Dolores is a professional ____. She plays the cello.
   Ⓐ physician
   Ⓑ musician
   Ⓒ engineer
   Ⓓ journalist

6. I'm a very good skater. ____ how to skate for a long time.
   Ⓐ I've known
   Ⓑ I know
   Ⓒ I knew
   Ⓓ I've knew

7. Sonia doesn't feel well. ____ a headache ____ early this morning.
   Ⓐ She had . . . since
   Ⓑ She's had . . . for
   Ⓒ She has . . . from
   Ⓓ She's had . . . since

8. A. How long ____ interested in science?
   B. ____ many years.
   Ⓐ are you . . . For
   Ⓑ you've been . . . Since
   Ⓒ have you been . . . For
   Ⓓ have you been . . . Since

9. A. Do you still drive a bus?
   B. No. ____ a bus for years. ____ a taxi now.
   Ⓐ I haven't driven . . . I drive
   Ⓑ I didn't drive . . . I've driven
   Ⓒ I don't drive . . . I drive
   Ⓓ I've driven . . . I've driven

10. Brian ____ the manager for a year. Before that, ____ the assistant manager.
    Ⓐ was been . . . he was
    Ⓑ has been . . . he's been
    Ⓒ is . . . he's been
    Ⓓ has been . . . he was

SKILLS CHECK

Match the "can do" statement and the correct sentence.

____ **1.** I can ask about the duration of an activity.
____ **2.** I can tell about the duration of an illness.
____ **3.** I can ask about a person's health.
____ **4.** I can describe an ailment or symptom.
____ **5.** I can ask about a person's skills.
____ **6.** I can ask about a person's interests.
____ **7.** I can tell about my work experience.
____ **8.** I can react to information.

a. How are you feeling today?
b. Are you interested in modern art?
c. Do you know how to ski?
d. How long have you owned this car?
e. Oh. I didn't know that.
f. I've been a taxi driver since 2009.
g. My neck is stiff.
h. I've been sick for three days.

Choose the correct answer.

1. Officer Martinez has been _____ traffic all morning.
   - (A) directing
   - (B) disturbing
   - (C) taking
   - (D) standing

2. I think the telephone is _____.
   - (A) talking
   - (B) ringing
   - (C) running
   - (D) barking

3. Our class is doing a chemistry _____ today.
   - (A) audience
   - (B) system
   - (C) experience
   - (D) experiment

4. I've worked here for a long time. I think it's time for me to ask my boss for a _____.
   - (A) raise
   - (B) job
   - (C) resume
   - (D) salary

5. Doctor Wu has _____ several babies today.
   - (A) given
   - (B) decided
   - (C) delivered
   - (D) assembled

6. _____ since last night.
   - (A) It's snowing
   - (B) It's been snowing
   - (C) It'll been snowing
   - (D) It snowed

7. How long _____ for the bus?
   - (A) did you been waiting
   - (B) have you been waiting
   - (C) you have been waiting
   - (D) are you been waiting

8. _____ in line for a long time?
   - (A) Are they standing
   - (B) Have been they standing
   - (C) Have they been stood
   - (D) Have they been standing

9. _____ e-mails for the past hour. Believe it or not, _____ more than 100 e-mails
   - (A) I've been writing . . . I've written
   - (B) I've been written . . . I've been writing
   - (C) I wrote . . . I written
   - (D) I've written . . . I'm writing

10. A. I'm nervous. _____ blood before.
    B. Really? _____ blood for years.
   - (A) I've been giving . . . I gave
   - (B) I didn't give . . . I'm giving
   - (C) I've never given . . . I've been giving
   - (D) I've never gave . . . I've been giving

SKILLS CHECK

Match the "can do" statement and the correct sentence.

_____ 1. I can ask about the duration of an activity.
_____ 2. I can tell about the duration of an activity.
_____ 3. I can report household repair problems.
_____ 4. I can describe tasks accomplished.
_____ 5. I can express surprise.
_____ 6. I can describe my feelings and emotions.
_____ 7. I can describe actions that haven't occurred yet.
_____ 8. I can reassure someone.

a. You're kidding!
b. Our bedroom ceiling has been leaking.
c. I'm nervous.
d. Don't worry!
e. How long have you been waiting?
f. I've never given blood before.
g. I've already made 75 pizzas.
h. We've been driving for five hours.

Choose the correct answer.

1. A. What do you like to do in your free time?
   B. I enjoy _____ the Web.
   Ⓐ traveling
   Ⓑ browsing
   Ⓒ watching
   Ⓓ following

2. It's impolite to _____ people while they're speaking.
   Ⓐ consider
   Ⓑ complain
   Ⓒ interrupt
   Ⓓ quit

3. I've been thinking about _____ my own business.
   Ⓐ starting
   Ⓑ going back
   Ⓒ keeping on
   Ⓓ liking

4. I'm considering _____ to technical school this fall.
   Ⓐ enrolling
   Ⓑ deciding
   Ⓒ practicing
   Ⓓ going

5. I just made an important _____. I'm going to retire this year.
   Ⓐ reason
   Ⓑ advice
   Ⓒ decision
   Ⓓ idea

6. I don't like _____ in the sun. I avoid _____ in the sun whenever I can.
   Ⓐ to sit . . . to sit
   Ⓑ sit . . . sitting
   Ⓒ sitting . . . to sit
   Ⓓ sitting . . . sitting

7. People think _____ is difficult. If you practice _____ a lot, you'll see that it isn't so difficult.
   Ⓐ skating . . . to skate
   Ⓑ to skate . . . skating
   Ⓒ skating . . . skating
   Ⓓ to skate . . . to skate

8. I started _____ when I was young, and _____ ever since.
   Ⓐ dancing . . . I'm dancing
   Ⓑ to dance . . . I've been dancing
   Ⓒ to dance . . . I danced
   Ⓓ dancing . . . I dance

9. I've decided _____ to Denver. I've been thinking about _____ there for a long time.
   Ⓐ to move . . . moving
   Ⓑ to move . . . to move
   Ⓒ moving . . . to move
   Ⓓ moving . . . moving

10. You need to quit _____. You can't keep on _____ for the rest of your life.
   Ⓐ complaining . . . to complain
   Ⓑ to complain . . . to complain
   Ⓒ complaining . . . complaining
   Ⓓ to complain . . . complaining

SKILLS CHECK

Match the "can do" statement and the correct sentence.

_____ 1. I can describe my recreation preferences.
_____ 2. I can introduce myself.
_____ 3. I can describe things I dislike doing.
_____ 4. I can offer advice.
_____ 5. I can ask if someone agrees.
_____ 6. I can agree with someone.
_____ 7. I can express appreciation.
_____ 8. I can tell about an important decision.

a. I avoid eating at fast-food restaurants.
b. Don't you think so?
c. That's very kind of you.
d. You're right.
e. Hello. My name is Howard.
f. I've decided to start my own business.
g. I really think you should stop eating junk food.
h. I enjoy painting.

CHAPTER 8

• Check-up Test • Skills Check

Choose the correct answer.

1. We need to _____ traveler's checks before our trip.
- Ⓐ rehearse
- Ⓑ send
- Ⓒ perform
- Ⓓ purchase

2. Do you and your friends enjoy _____ politics?
- Ⓐ discussing
- Ⓑ realizing
- Ⓒ believing
- Ⓓ memorizing

3. We were very upset when we arrived at the airport. Our plane had already _____.
- Ⓐ sailed away
- Ⓑ gone by
- Ⓒ taken off
- Ⓓ started

4. Please call a doctor! I think I just _____ my wrist.
- Ⓐ packed
- Ⓑ sprained
- Ⓒ passed by
- Ⓓ bumped into

5. Professor Walters was angry. The university decided to _____ his lecture.
- Ⓐ call
- Ⓑ twist
- Ⓒ dislocate
- Ⓓ cancel

6. Howard _____ his green striped tie to work yesterday because _____ it the day before.
- Ⓐ didn't wear . . . he had worn
- Ⓑ didn't wear . . . he's worn
- Ⓒ hasn't worn . . . he wore
- Ⓓ hadn't worn . . . he had worn

7. By the time I _____ to the train, it _____.
- Ⓐ gotten . . . had already left
- Ⓑ got . . . has already left
- Ⓒ have gotten . . . already left
- Ⓓ got . . . had already left

8. We enjoyed _____ dessert last night. We _____ dessert in a long time.
- Ⓐ to have . . . haven't had
- Ⓑ having . . . hadn't had
- Ⓒ to have had . . . hadn't had
- Ⓓ to have . . . didn't have

9. Rita hurt herself while she _____ last week. She _____ before.
- Ⓐ skied . . . didn't ski
- Ⓑ was skiing . . . had never skied
- Ⓒ has skied . . . wasn't skiing
- Ⓓ has been skiing . . . hadn't skied

10. We were surprised that Tim and Tina broke up. They _____ for years, and Tim _____ Tina a beautiful engagement ring.
- Ⓐ went out . . . has been buying
- Ⓑ had gone out . . . had been buying
- Ⓒ had been going out . . . had bought
- Ⓓ have been going out . . . was buying

SKILLS CHECK

Match the "can do" statement and the correct sentence.

_____ **1.** I can describe things I had already done before.

_____ **2.** I can describe the consequences of being late.

_____ **3.** I can describe forgetting to do something.

_____ **4.** I can describe feelings and emotions.

_____ **5.** I can share news about someone.

_____ **6.** I can react to bad news.

_____ **7.** I can describe an accomplishment.

a. That's terrible!

b. I had driven to the beach the weekend before.

c. Have you heard about Harry?

d. I got a promotion last week.

e. I had forgotten to turn on the oven.

f. By the time I got to the library, it had already closed.

g. I was furious.

Choose the correct answer.

1. Could you possibly help me ____ my new computer?
   - Ⓐ hear from
   - Ⓑ hang up
   - Ⓒ hook up
   - Ⓓ hand in

2. Do you have a dictionary? I need to ____ a word I don't know.
   - Ⓐ look through
   - Ⓑ look up
   - Ⓒ look up to
   - Ⓓ call on

3. I'm going to ____ my clothes at the cleaner's this morning.
   - Ⓐ pick up
   - Ⓑ pick on
   - Ⓒ pick out
   - Ⓓ put away

4. Please ____ the garbage before you leave for work.
   - Ⓐ take after
   - Ⓑ take back
   - Ⓒ take out
   - Ⓓ take off

5. It's very hot today. Let's ____ the air conditioner all afternoon.
   - Ⓐ drop off
   - Ⓑ use up
   - Ⓒ do over
   - Ⓓ leave on

6. A. Did you remember to ____ the alarm?
   B. I forgot! I'll ____ right away!
   - Ⓐ turn on . . . turn on it
   - Ⓑ turn it on . . . turn on
   - Ⓒ turn on . . . turn it on
   - Ⓓ turn on it . . . turn it

7. You need to ____ and ____.
   - Ⓐ fill out this . . . hand in it
   - Ⓑ fill this out . . . hand it in
   - Ⓒ fill out this . . . hand it in
   - Ⓓ fill this out . . . hand in it

8. Nancy handed in her composition, but the teacher ____.
   - Ⓐ gave her it back
   - Ⓑ gave back it to her
   - Ⓒ gave it back to her
   - Ⓓ gave back to her it

9. I hadn't ____ for many years, and then last week I ____ at the supermarket.
   - Ⓐ heard from him . . . ran him into
   - Ⓑ heard from him . . . ran into him
   - Ⓒ heard him from . . . ran him into
   - Ⓓ heard him from . . . ran into him

10. A. Can you help me? I'm ____.
    B. Here's a nice suit. ____.
    - Ⓐ looking for a suit . . . Try on it
    - Ⓑ looking a suit for . . . Try on it
    - Ⓒ looking a suit for . . . Try it on
    - Ⓓ looking for a suit . . . Try it on

SKILLS CHECK

Match the "can do" statement and the correct sentence.

____ 1. I can ask about future plans.
____ 2. I can tell about future plans.
____ 3. I can ask if someone remembered to do something.
____ 4. I can describe forgetting to do something.
____ 5. I can express obligation.
____ 6. I can give advice.
____ 7. I can invite someone to do something.

a. I forgot!
b. I have to fill out my income tax form.
c. Would you like to get together today?
d. When are you going to hook up your new computer?
e. Did you remember to turn on the alarm?
f. I think you should throw them away.
g. I'm going to call him up sometime next week.

Choose the correct answer.

1. This table is very expensive. I don't think we can ____ it.
   Ⓐ allow
   Ⓑ afford
   Ⓒ spend
   Ⓓ support

2. Marco plays soccer very well. He's very ____.
   Ⓐ athletic
   Ⓑ available
   Ⓒ compatible
   Ⓓ lenient

3. Our family is very ____ about the environment.
   Ⓐ opposed
   Ⓑ allergic
   Ⓒ concerned
   Ⓓ similar

4. My sister likes science, and so do I. We have the same academic ____.
   Ⓐ instructions
   Ⓑ decisions
   Ⓒ collections
   Ⓓ interests

5. It's important to ____ when the teacher is talking.
   Ⓐ explain
   Ⓑ respect
   Ⓒ pay attention
   Ⓓ express

6. A. I'll be out of town next week.
   B. What a coincidence! ____
   Ⓐ So I will.
   Ⓑ Will I, too.
   Ⓒ So will I.
   Ⓓ I too will.

7. A. I haven't finished my composition yet.
   B. What a coincidence! ____
   Ⓐ I haven't neither.
   Ⓑ Neither haven't I.
   Ⓒ Either haven't I.
   Ⓓ Neither have I.

8. A. Why are those two customers arguing?
   B. He wants to buy that lamp, ____.
   Ⓐ and she does, too
   Ⓑ and so she does
   Ⓒ and so she, too
   Ⓓ and does she, too

9. Betty and her husband were late for work because she didn't hear the alarm, ____.
   Ⓐ and he didn't neither
   Ⓑ and either didn't he
   Ⓒ and neither did he
   Ⓓ and either he didn't

10. A. Can you possibly work late tonight?
    B. I can't, ____.
    Ⓐ and my brother can
    Ⓑ but my brother can
    Ⓒ and neither can't my brother
    Ⓓ but my brother can't either

SKILLS CHECK

Match the "can do" statement and the correct sentence.

____ 1. I can give information about myself.
____ 2. I can ask for a reason.
____ 3. I can describe a person's background.
____ 4. I can describe a person's interests.
____ 5. I can describe a person's personality.
____ 6. I can describe things that haven't occurred yet.
____ 7. I can offer a suggestion.

a. She enjoys working with computers.
b. They've never been on a roller coaster before.
c. He's shy and quiet.
d. Why can't you help me with the dishes?
e. You should ask her.
f. I'm allergic to cats.
g. She grew up in a small town in the South.

APPENDIX

Listening Scripts

Chapter 1 – Page 6

Listen and choose the correct answer.

1. What are you doing?
2. Do you watch the news very often?
3. Are you a good swimmer?
4. What's Cathy reading?
5. Who cooks in your family?
6. Do they like to skate?
7. Does your sister want to be a ballet dancer?
8. Do you and your friends play basketball very often?
9. Are your parents good dancers?
10. What does Peter want to be when he grows up?

Chapter 2 – Page 17

Listen and choose the correct answer.

1. Did you do well at your job interview yesterday?
2. Were your children tired last night?
3. What was he doing when he broke his leg?
4. Did you finish your dinner last night?
5. How did your husband lose his wallet?
6. What was your supervisor doing?
7. Did you do well on the exam?
8. What happened while you were preparing lunch?

Chapter 3 – Page 24

Listen to the conversation and choose the answer that is true.

1. A. Are you going to wear your brown suit today?
   B. No, I don't think so. I wore my brown suit yesterday. I'm going to wear my gray suit.
2. A. Let's make beef stew for dinner!
   B. But we had that last week. Let's make spaghetti and meatballs instead.
   A. Okay.
3. A. Do you want to watch the game show on Channel 5 or the news program on Channel 9?
   B. Let's watch the news program.
4. A. What's the matter with it?
   B. The brakes don't work, and it doesn't start very well in the morning.
5. A. What are you going to do tomorrow?
   B. I'm going to plant carrots, tomatoes, and lettuce.
6. A. This computer is very powerful, but it's too expensive.
   B. You're right.

Side by Side Gazette – Page 35

Listen to the messages on Dave's machine. Match the messages.

You have five messages.

Message Number One: "Hi, Dave. It's Sarah. Thanks for the invitation, but I can't come to your party tomorrow. I'll be taking my uncle to the hospital. Maybe next time." [beep]

Message Number Two: "Hello, Dave. It's Bob. I'm sorry that my wife and I won't be able to come to your party tomorrow. We'll be attending a wedding out of town. I hope it's a great party. Have fun!" [beep]

Message Number Three: "Dave? It's Paula. How's it going? I got your message about the party tomorrow. Unfortunately, I won't be able to go. I'll be studying all weekend. Talk to you soon." [beep]

Message Number Four: "Hi, Dave. It's Joe. Thanks for the invitation to your party. I'll be visiting my parents in New York City, so I'm afraid I won't be around. I'll call you when I get back." [beep]

Message Number Five: "Hello, Dave? It's Carla. Thanks for the invitation to your party. I don't have anything to do tomorrow night, so I'll definitely be there. I'm really looking forward to it. See you tomorrow." [beep]

Chapter 4 – Page 49

1. *Linda is on vacation in San Francisco. This is her list of things to do. Check the things on the list Linda has already done.*

   Linda has already seen the Golden Gate Bridge. She hasn't visited Golden Gate Park yet. She took a tour of Alcatraz Prison yesterday. She's going to go to Chinatown tomorrow. She hasn't ridden a cable car yet. She's eaten at Fisherman's Wharf, but she hasn't had time to buy souvenirs.

2. *Alan is a secretary in a very busy office. This is his list of things to do before 5 P.M. on Friday. Check the things on the list Alan has already done.*

   Alan has already called Mrs. Porter. He has to type the letter to the Mervis Company. He hasn't taken the mail to the post office yet. He's gone to the bank. He hasn't sent an e-mail to the company's office in Denver, and he's going to speak to the boss about his salary next week.

3. *It's Saturday, and Judy and Paul Johnson are doing lots of things around the house. This is the list of things they have to do today. Check the things on the list they've already done.*

   Judy and Paul haven't done the laundry. They have to wash the kitchen windows. They've paid the bills. They haven't given the dog a bath. They'll clean the garage later. They couldn't fix the bathroom sink or repair the fence, but they vacuumed the living room rug.

Chapter 5 – Page 60

Listen to the conversation and choose the answer that is true.

1. A. How long have you had a backache?
   B. For three days.
2. A. Has your father always been an engineer?
   B. No, he hasn't.
3. A. How long has your knee been swollen?
   B. For a week.
4. A. How long have you known how to ski?
   B. Since I was a teenager.
5. A. Did you live in Tokyo for a long time?
   B. Yes. Five years.
6. A. How long has Roger been interested in Egyptian history?
   B. Since he lived in Cairo.
7. A. Is Amy still in the hospital?
   B. Oh. I forgot to tell you. She's been home for two days.
8. A. Have you played hockey for a long time?
   B. Yes. I've played hockey since I moved to Toronto three years ago.

Side by Side Gazette – Page 67

Listen to the voice-mail messages between Gloria Rivera and her office assistant, Sam. Has Sam done the things on Ms. Rivera's list? Check Yes or No.

You have one message. Tuesday, 8:15 A.M.

Hello, Sam? This is Ms. Rivera. I'll be out of the office all day today. I'm not feeling well. Here's a list of things you'll need to do while I'm not here. First, please write a note to Mrs. Wilson and tell her I'm sick. Then, please call Mr. Chen and change the time of our appointment. Also, send an e-mail to everybody in the office, and tell them about next week's meeting. Don't forget to speak to the custodian about my broken desk lamp. I hope he can fix it. Hmm. Let's see. I know there are a few more things. Oh, yes. Please make a list of all the employees and give it to Ms. Baxter. She asked me for the list last week. Okay, Sam. I think that's everything. Oh . . . one more thing. Please take the package on my desk to the post office if you have time. And that's it. Thanks, Sam. I'll see you tomorrow morning.

You have reached the voice mailbox of Gloria Rivera. Please leave a message after the tone.

Ms. Rivera? This is Sam. I'm sorry you aren't feeling well. I hope you feel better tomorrow. I'm calling to tell you what I've done today, and what I haven't done yet. It's been very busy here, so I haven't had time to do everything. I wrote a note to Mrs. Wilson. I called Mr. Chen and changed the time of your appointment. I also sent the e-mail about next week's meeting. I haven't spoken to the custodian. He's been sick all week. I made a list of all the employees, but I haven't given it to Ms. Baxter yet. I'll give it to her early tomorrow morning. Finally, I haven't taken the package to the post office yet. I haven't had time. I'm going to take it to the post office on my way home. Again, I hope you're feeling better. I'll see you in the morning.

Chapter 6 – Page 79

Which Word Do You Hear?

Listen and choose the correct answer.

1. He's gone to the bank.
2. I've never written so many letters in one day before.
3. She's been seeing patients all day.
4. What courses have you taken this year?
5. Is Beverly giving blood?
6. Ben has driven all night.

Who Is Speaking?

Listen and decide who is speaking.

1. What a day! All the tenants have been complaining that nothing is working.
2. I'm very tired. I've given six lessons today.
3. Thank you! You've been a wonderful audience!
4. I'm really tired. I've been watching them all day.
5. I'm very tired. I've been looking at paychecks since early this morning.
6. It's been a long day. I've been selling tickets since ten A.M.

Chapter 7 – Page 93

Listen and choose the correct answer.

1. **A.** I avoid going to the mall whenever I can.
   B. Me, too.
2. **A.** I've decided to sell my car.
   B. Your beautiful car?
3. **A.** Please try to quit biting your nails.
   B. Okay. Mom.
4. **A.** Do you enjoy traveling by plane?
   B. Very much.
5. **A.** We're thinking about moving to Florida.
   B. Oh. That's interesting.
6. **A.** I've been considering getting married for a long time.
   B. Oh, really? I didn't know that.
7. **A.** Don't stop practicing.
   B. Okay.
8. **A.** Interrupting people is a habit I just can't break.
   B. That's too bad.

Chapter 8 – Page 103

Listen and choose the correct answer.

1. Did your parents enjoy eating at Joe's Restaurant last night?
2. Why don't you want to see the new James Bond movie with us next weekend?
3. Did you get to the play on time last night?
4. Michael, please go upstairs and do your homework.
5. Why did Carmen do so well on the history test?
6. We really enjoyed our vacation at the Ritz Hotel.

Side by Side Gazette – Page 113

Listen to the Olympic Game highlights. Match the highlight and the sport.

And now, sports fans, let's finish today's program with highlights of the Olympic Games. Here are five of my favorite moments in the most recent summer and winter games:

There are three seconds left in the game. Number 38 gets ready to shoot again. His team needs this point to win the game. He shoots, and it's in the basket! [Buzzer] That's it! The game is over! And the United States wins 99 to 98. The U.S. gets the gold medal!

Kirshner is still in front. But wait! Look at Tanaka in the next lane! What speed! Look at him move through the water! Tanaka is even with Kirshner. Now Tanaka is ahead! And Tanaka wins the event! Japan wins the gold medal, Germany gets the silver, and Hungary gets the bronze.

Natasha knows she must do this floor routine perfectly to win the gold medal. She had problems today when she fell off the balance beam, and that's usually her best event. She's doing very well. What a strong and graceful athlete! And here's the most difficult part of her routine. Beautiful! But, oh . . . she falls! Natasha has fallen at the very end of her routine. What a shame! There will be no gold for Natasha this year.

What a race! Anderson is still in first place and Sanchez is right behind him in second place. Look at Sanchez run! He's moving ahead of Anderson. The lead has changed! Sanchez is now in front! He crosses the finish line! Sanchez wins with a time of two hours, ten minutes, and eleven seconds. So Mexico wins the gold, Canada gets the silver, and France gets the bronze.

And Tamara leaves the ice after a beautiful long program! I think that's one of the best programs I've ever seen at the Olympics. She moved so gracefully to the music. Let's see what the judges think. Look at these marks! Five-point-eight, five-point-nine, five-point-nine, five-point-eight, five-point-seven, five-point-nine, five-point-nine, six-point-oh, five-point-eight. Excellent scores! Tamara wins the gold medal! Look at all the flowers people are throwing on the ice! I'm sure this is the happiest day of Tamara's life!

Chapter 9 – Page 129

Listen and choose what the people are talking about.

1. **A.** Where can I try them on?
   B. The dressing room is over there.
2. **A.** Now remember, you can't bring them back!
   B. I understand.
3. **A.** Have you filled it out yet?
   B. No. I'm having some trouble. Can you help me?
4. **A.** Please drop them off at the school by eight o'clock.
   B. By eight o'clock? Okay.
5. **A.** Where should I hang them?
   B. What about over the fireplace?
6. **A.** Have you thought it over?
   B. Yes, I have.
7. **A.** It's cold in here.
   B. You're right. I'll turn it on.
8. **A.** Should we use it up?
   B. No. Let's throw it out.
9. **A.** What are you going to do?
   B. I'm going to turn it down.

Chapter 10 – p. 137

Listen and choose what the people are talking about.

1. **A.** To tell the truth, I'm a little shy.
   B. What a coincidence! I am, too.
2. **A.** I enjoy going to plays and concerts.
   B. We're very compatible. So do I.
3. **A.** I'm enjoying this course.
   B. I am, too.
4. **A.** I'm from Minnesota.
   B. That's interesting. So am I.
5. **A.** I go swimming three times a week.
   B. What a coincidence! I do, too.
6. **A.** I'm opposed to using animals in scientific experiments.
   B. I am, too.

Side by Side Gazette – Page 148

Listen to the messages on Mary and Jim's answering machines. Answer true or false.

[*Monday, 6:15* P.M.]

Hi, Mary. It's Jim. Are you by any chance interested in going to a jazz concert this Friday night? Please call me and let me know. Talk to you later.

[*Monday, 9:13* P.M.]

Hi, Jim. It's Mary. I'm returning your call. Thanks for the invitation. I know you like jazz, and I do, too. And I'd really like to go to the concert with you, but I have to work this Friday night. Do you want to play tennis on Saturday afternoon? Let me know. 'Bye.

[*Tuesday, 3:40* P.M.]

Hi, Mary. It's Jim. I'm sorry I missed your call last night. I was at the laundromat, and I got home very late. I'm free on Saturday, but unfortunately, I really don't like to play tennis. Actually, I'm a very bad tennis player. Do you want to go to the ballet with me on Saturday night? Let me know, and I'll order tickets. Talk to you soon.

[*Wednesday, 5:50* P.M.]

Hi, Jim. It's Mary. I got your message. Believe it or not, I've already gone to the ballet this week. I went with my sister last night. I have an idea! Let's see the new Steven Steelberg movie. I hear that it's great. Call and let me know.

[*Thursday, 6:30* P.M.]

Hi, Mary. It's Jim. Sorry I missed your call again. I guess we're playing "telephone tag!" The movie sounds great. I haven't seen it yet. Do you want to have dinner before the movie? There's a wonderful new Italian restaurant downtown. Let me know. 'Bye.

[*Friday, 5:17* P.M.]

Hi, Jim. Guess who! You won't believe it! I just found out that I have to work this Saturday night. It's a shame because I really wanted to see that movie. I'm not busy on Sunday. Are you free on Sunday afternoon? Let me know. By the way, I don't really like Italian food very much. There's a very good Greek restaurant in my neighborhood. Maybe we can have dinner there after the movie. What do you think? Talk to you later.

Thematic Glossary

Actions and Activities

Ailments, Symptoms, and Injuries

Clothing

Computers

Days of the Week 7

Describing with Adjectives

Describing with Adverbs

Events

Parts of the Body

People

Personal Information

Places

School

Seasons 7

Sports

Time Expressions

Transportation

Work

Irregular Verbs

be	was/were	been
become	became	become
begin	began	begun
bite	bit	bitten
blow	blew	blown
break	broke	broken
bring	brought	brought
build	built	built
buy	bought	bought
catch	caught	caught
choose	chose	chosen
come	came	come
cost	cost	cost
cut	cut	cut
do	did	done
draw	drew	drawn
drink	drank	drunk
drive	drove	driven
eat	ate	eaten
fall	fell	fallen
feed	fed	fed
feel	felt	felt
fight	fought	fought
find	found	found
fit	fit	fit
fly	flew	flown
forget	forgot	forgotten
forgive	forgave	forgiven
freeze	froze	frozen
get	got	gotten
give	gave	given
go	went	gone
grow	grew	grown
hang	hung	hung
have	had	had
hear	heard	heard
hide	hid	hidden
hit	hit	hit
hold	held	held
hurt	hurt	hurt
keep	kept	kept
know	knew	known
lead	led	led
leave	left	left
lend	lent	lent
let	let	let
light	lit	lit
lose	lost	lost
make	made	made
mean	meant	meant
meet	met	met
put	put	put
quit	quit	quit
read	read	read
ride	rode	ridden
ring	rang	rung
run	ran	run
say	said	said
see	saw	seen
sell	sold	sold
send	sent	sent
set	set	set
sew	sewed	sewed/sewn
shake	shook	shaken
shrink	shrank	shrunk
sing	sang	sung
sit	sat	sat
sleep	slept	slept
speak	spoke	spoken
spend	spent	spent
stand	stood	stood
steal	stole	stolen
sweep	swept	swept
swim	swam	swum
take	took	taken
teach	taught	taught
tell	told	told
think	thought	thought
throw	threw	thrown
understand	understood	understood
wake	woke	woken
wear	wore	worn
win	won	won
wind	wound	wound
write	wrote	written

Index